Quarterly Essay

CONTENTS

1   BAD NEWS

Murdoch's *Australian* and the Shaping of the Nation

Robert Manne

120   CORRESPONDENCE

John van Tiggelen, Eric Knight, Jon Altman, Linda Botterill,
Tim Mather, Bernard Salt, Judith Brett

141   Contributors

Quarterly Essay is published four times a year by Black Inc., an imprint of Schwartz Media Pty Ltd. Publisher: Morry Schwartz.

ISBN 978-1-86395-544-7 ISSN 1832-0953

ALL RIGHTS RESERVED.
No part of this publication may be reproduced, stored in a retrieval system, or transmitted in any form by any means electronic, mechanical, photocopying, recording or otherwise without the prior consent of the publishers.

Essay & correspondence © retained by the authors.

Subscriptions – 1 year (4 issues): $49 within Australia incl. GST. Outside Australia $79. 2 years (8 issues): $95 within Australia incl. GST. Outside Australia $155.

Payment may be made by MasterCard or Visa, or by cheque made out to Schwartz Media. Payment includes postage and handling.

To subscribe, fill out and post the subscription card or form inside this issue, or subscribe online:

www.quarterlyessay.com
subscribe@blackincbooks.com
Phone: 61 3 9486 0288

Correspondence should be addressed to:

The Editor, Quarterly Essay
37–39 Langridge Street
Collingwood VIC 3066 Australia
Phone: 61 3 9486 0288 / Fax: 61 3 9486 0244
Email: quarterlyessay@blackincbooks.com

Editor: Chris Feik. Management: Sophy Williams, Caitlin Yates. Publicity: Elisabeth Young. Design: Guy Mirabella. Assistant Editor/Production Coordinator: Nikola Lusk. Typesetting: Duncan Blachford.

Printed by Griffin Press, Australia. The paper used to produce this book comes from wood grown in sustainable forests.

BAD NEWS

Murdoch's Australian *and*
the Shaping of the Nation

Robert Manne

When I decided to write this essay, the Murdoch global media empire was in rude health. By the time it was completed, the empire was badly weakened. The collapse of an empire is frequently triggered by a small event. In this case it was the revulsion felt by the British public after the discovery that reporters at the Murdoch tabloid *News of the World* had hacked into the mobile phone of a kidnapped thirteen-year-old girl later found murdered. Because of a *Guardian* investigation, the British public learned that phone hacking was a common practice at *News of the World*. Les Hinton, the chairman of News International at the time of the hacking, resigned. Both Rebekah Brooks, the head of Murdoch's newspaper division in the United Kingdom, and Andy Coulson, a former editor of *News of the World*, were arrested. Conspiracies often begin to unravel when conspirators turn against each other. James Murdoch, chairman of News International, gave evidence to a House of Commons committee. James assured the committee that he had believed only one journalist was involved in phone hacking when he signed a cheque for £700,000 in favour of a victim. Two disgraced News International employees, Tom Crone and Colin Myler, claimed that this was not true. They had shown him an email that revealed a widespread practice of hacking at *News of the World*. If James Murdoch is unable to disprove their allegation, his future at News is in doubt. Even more seriously, if it can be shown that Rupert Murdoch was told about the phone hacking by his son, his credibility would not easily recover. As I write, Rupert Murdoch's control of his empire is shaky.

Rupert Murdoch is one of the most powerful people in the English-speaking democracies. His genius has been to discover different ways in which his two passions – a desire for money and a thirst for power – can be combined. In the United States, Fox News is not only one of his most profitable businesses. It has gained a great influence over the choice of Republican Party candidate for the presidency and has injected into the bloodstream of American political culture the poison of a strident populist conservatism. In Britain, somewhat differently, Rupert Murdoch has used his newspaper power to instil a fear into prime ministers and leaders of the Opposition, in part at least to advance his other, more lucrative, commercial interests. In Australia, the country of his birth for which he seems to feel an especial responsibility, he has discovered how to use the 70 per cent of the national and statewide press he owns to ensure that the values drawn from his right-wing political philosophy remain dominant within the political mainstream. Murdoch has presented a major problem for the democratic cultures of three Anglophone countries. In America it is Fox News, in Britain News International's tabloid culture, and in Australia the direct political influence of his newspapers. For the moment Murdoch's power has diminished, whether permanently or temporarily it is too early to say. Politicians who once courted him are now in flight. This situation provides an unexpectedly propitious climate for the evaluation of the political influence and the character of his most important political asset in this country, the broadsheet he created in 1964, the *Australian*.

I took the decision to write this essay in September 2010. I had long been concerned with the role the *Australian* had played over the question of action on climate change. By then I was also convinced that this newspaper, which had played an important part in the unravelling of the Rudd government, would not rest until it saw the end of the Gillard government and the destruction of the Labor–Greens alliance. However, there was more to the decision than this.

The *Australian* is in my view the country's most important newspaper. Under Chris Mitchell it has evolved into a kind of broadsheet perhaps never before seen here. It is an unusually ideological paper, committed to advancing the causes of neoliberalism in economics and neoconservatism in the sphere of foreign policy. Its style and tone are also unlike that of any other newspaper in the nation's history. The *Australian* is ruthless in pursuit of those who oppose its worldview – market fundamentalism, minimal action on climate change, the federal Intervention in indigenous affairs, uncritical support for the American alliance and for Israel, opposition to what it calls political correctness and moral relativism. It exhibits distaste, even hatred, for what it terms "the Left," and in particular for the Greens. It is driven by contempt for its two natural rivals, the Fairfax press and the ABC, one of which it seems to wish to destroy altogether, the other of which it seeks to discredit for its supposed left-wing bias and to reshape. Both the Fairfax newspapers and the ABC are constantly attacked and belittled by the *Australian*. Yet at least until the Murdoch empire was weakened in early July 2011, for the most part they turned the other cheek.

The *Australian* is a remorseless campaigning paper; in recent times against the Building the Education Revolution program and the National Broadband Network. In these campaigns its assigned journalists appear to begin with their editorially determined conclusion and then to seek out evidence to support it. The paper is also unusually self-referential and boastful, heaping extravagant praise upon itself for its acumen and prescience almost on a daily basis, never failing to inform its readers that it was the first to report something or the only paper to provide real scrutiny or intelligent interpretation. Related to its boastfulness is the *Australian's* notorious sensitivity to criticism. It regularly explodes with indignation and rage when criticised. It also bears many grudges. The *Australian* never forgave former Victorian police commissioner Simon Overland, who once had the temerity to complain about its behaviour on the eve of an anti-terrorist raid in Melbourne. It did not rest until his career was ruined. Not even then. It also has an intensely aggressive culture, described to me by close observers as bullying or swaggering or macho. Chris Mitchell is determined that his paper will be talked about, a style that his editor, Clive Mathieson, described vividly in an interview with me as "elbows out." In no other newspaper is the spirit of the editor so omnipresent, either directly through the editorials – the daily morning missives to the nation which he inspires – or indirectly throughout its pages. Mitchell is frequently interviewed by his own journalists. He uses those he most trusts to fight his battles with his many enemies. In a recent profile of him written by Sally Neighbour for the *Monthly*, David Marr described his uncanny ability to personalise everything he deals with as his peculiar "genius." Because of the charismatic authority over his journalists exercised by Mitchell, and because of the costs that are paid by anyone in his paper who defies him, one very senior journalist likened the atmosphere inside the *Australian* to that of a cult.

The *Australian* is this country's only genuinely national general newspaper, with a readership in every state and territory and in the capital cities, the regional towns and rural areas. Although its weekday sales are small – somewhere between 100,000 and 130,000 – it is extremely well resourced by its proprietor, able to employ many of Australia's best journalists. As a consequence, as I learned in interviews with Senator Bob Brown and with senior members of the Gillard government, the *Australian* now dominates the Canberra press gallery not only in the number of journalists employed – at some press conferences half of those attending are from the *Australian* – but also in the aggression its reporters display and their capacity for teamwork in pursuit of their prey. Because of the dominant position it has assumed in its Canberra coverage, the *Australian* influences the way the much more widely read News Limited tabloids, like the *Daily Telegraph* and the *Herald Sun*, report national politics and frequently sets the agenda of commercial radio and television and the ABC, even the upmarket breakfast program on Radio National. The *Australian* is in addition the only newspaper that is read by virtually all members of the group of insiders I call the political class, a group that includes politicians, leading public servants, business people and the most politically engaged citizens. Even those members of the political class who loathe the paper understand that they cannot afford to ignore it. Most importantly of all, as Mark Latham pointed out in a recent article in the *Australian Financial Review*, the *Australian* has now transcended the traditional newspaper role of reporter or analyst and become an active player in both federal and state politics. As such it exercises what Stanley Baldwin once called, in describing the influence of the great press barons of his era, "power without responsibility."

An analysis of the role the *Australian* has played in helping to shape values and to influence national political life during the period of the Chris Mitchell editorship (which began in mid-2002) is thus long overdue. There is, however, little point in outlining the nation's problem with the *Australian* generally or abstractly. Both its overbearing character and its unhealthy influence must be demonstrated. That is what I hope in this essay to be able to do through a series of detailed case studies – concerning the revisionist history of Keith Windschuttle, the invasion of Iraq, the criticism of the paper offered by *Media Watch*, the question of global warming, the rise and fall of Kevin Rudd, the Julie Posetti and the Larissa Behrendt affairs, and the rise of the Greens.

Under Chris Mitchell the *Australian* has become one of the most important political forces in the country. No realistic account of power in contemporary Australia can afford to ignore it.

Australia was founded on the basis of the destruction of Aboriginal society. As a result, no question has so haunted the national imagination. During the course of the long dispossession, historians described the process of destruction with emotions ranging from racist denigration and callous indifference to genuine pity. Following the dispossession, as the anthropologist W.E.H. Stanner was the first to observe, the story of the destruction of Aboriginal society was excised from the history books in a psychologically complex process he described as "the great Australian silence." Australia became "the quiet continent." In the creation of the nation "no blood had been spilt." It was only in the late 1960s and beyond – through the seminal Boyer Lectures delivered by Stanner, through the groundbreaking trilogy on the dispossession and its aftermath by the great scholar C.D. Rowley, and through the many books of Henry Reynolds – that the destruction of Aboriginal society returned from the period of repression to become a central question of Australian history.

In late 2002 Keith Windschuttle published the first volume of *The Fabrication of Aboriginal History*. The book represented the first substantial challenge from the Right to the understanding of the meaning of the dispossession that had transformed national consciousness from the 1960s. Windschuttle chose to begin his history with Tasmania, where between 1803 and 1834 the entire "full-blood" indigenous population, thought by scholars to have numbered about 4000 or 5000 people, had either died or been exiled to Flinders Island. Tasmania was an interesting choice for the first volume. During the nineteenth and early twentieth centuries the fate of the indigenous Tasmanians had stirred the European moral imagination more profoundly than that of any other indigenous Australian group. In 1943 Raphael Lemkin, the Polish-Jewish jurist, coined a legal term for the idea of the total destruction of a people: genocide. Lemkin himself wrote extensively on the question of the destruction of the Tasmanian Aborigines. Before Windschuttle published the first volume of his *Fabrication*, not only in the scholarly textbooks but also in common understanding in Australia and beyond, the idea that the Tasmanian Aborigines had suffered genocide was an almost uncontested common wisdom. Oddly enough, the conventional idea that the Tasmanian Aborigines had been the victims of a successful genocide was resisted by two of the scholars Windschuttle had most firmly in his sights. In *The Aboriginal Tasmanians*, Lyndall Ryan claimed that the "conscious policy of genocide" had failed. Quite differently, in *An Indelible Stain?*, Henry Reynolds argued that in Tasmania there had been no British government policy of genocide.

In *Fabrication* Windschuttle argued that in the British settlement of Tasmania a mere 118 Aborigines had been killed. Far from it being a case of genocide, as the left-wing fabricators of Aboriginal history supposedly claimed, Windschuttle argued that the establishment of the colony was one of the most gentle in the history of the British Empire. There had been no Black War. The Aborigines had no concept of land or property. Their misguided attacks on the British settlers were nothing more than criminal acts motivated exclusively by the desire for consumer goods. Windschuttle could not deny that thirty years after the arrival of the British almost all the original indigenous people had died, with a tiny remnant exiled to Flinders Island. He attributed their sudden demise to their susceptibility to introduced disease and to the willingness of the menfolk to prostitute their women by handing them over to the British arrivals. Unhappily, the Tasmanians were so backward a people that they were unable to generate a leadership wise enough to renounce their ancient way of life following the arrival of the British settlers and seize the bounty of British civilisation so generously offered them. This summary might appear a parody of Windschuttle's argument. It is not.

Keith Windschuttle is not a fool. In his attack on earlier scholarship he landed some powerful blows. Nonetheless, the scholarship displayed in *Fabrication* was frequently of an altogether risible kind. Windschuttle argued that the Aboriginal Tasmanians had no concept of land or property. As Henry Reynolds has pointed out, he was unaware that the most important Tasmanian Aboriginal dictionary lists no fewer than twenty words for "country." To show that the Tasmanian Aborigines had no grounds for complaint over food supply, Windschuttle argued that the British settlers stopped hunting native birds and animals in 1811. As James Boyce has shown, in fact an orgy of hunting continued for decades longer. Most importantly of all, Windschuttle's claim that it is "clear" that a mere 118 Aborigines died a violent death at British hands (later revised to 120) is based on two propositions that would not pass the historian's "laugh test," namely that every Aboriginal death at British settler hands must be recorded in an extant document and that, after battle, no Aborigine ever died of wounds.

Even worse than the inadequacy of the scholarship, however, was the complete absence in Windschuttle of a sense of tragedy in the telling of his story, which gave the book a coldness. Compare words taken from the concluding passage in John West's *A History of Tasmania* published in 1852 with a concluding passage of Keith Windschuttle's *Fabrication of Aboriginal History*.

> [The colonists] are charmed by their simplicity; they sleep among them without fear: but these notes soon change; and passing from censure to hatred, they speak of them as improvident, importunate, and intrusive; as rapacious and mischievous; then as treacherous and blood-thirsty ... At length the secret comes out; the tribe which welcomed the first settler with shouts and dancing ... has ceased to live ... It was, indeed, a mournful spectacle: the last Tasmanian quitting the shores of his ancestors! Forty years before, the first settler had erected his encampment! A change so rapid in the relations of a people to the soil, will scarcely find a parallel in this world's history ... – John West

> [W]e should see them as active agents of their own demise ... The real tragedy of the Aborigines was not British colonization per se but that their society was, on the one hand, so internally dysfunctional

and, on the other hand, so incompatible with the looming presence of the rest of the world … They had survived for millennia it is true, but it seems clear that this owed more to good fortune than to good management. The "slow strangulation of the mind" was true not only of their technical abilities but also of their social relationships. Hence, it was not surprising that when the British arrived, this small, precarious society quickly collapsed under the dual weight of the susceptibility of its members to disease and the abuse and neglect of its women. – Keith Windschuttle

It is very unusual for books in the humanities to become topics of the kind of extended national conversation only daily newspapers can sustain. Windschuttle's scholarship was slipshod. His understanding of the tragedy that had overtaken the indigenous people of Tasmania compared unfavourably with a book written a century and a half earlier. Its enthusiastic reception needs to be explained.

The process of turning *Fabrication* into a major national event began at Chris Mitchell's *Australian*. On the eve of its publication, Bernard Lane, the journalist assigned to cover the controversy, penned a flattering portrait of Windschuttle. This was followed by a column in which Windschuttle outlined his views. When Windschuttle's book was launched by Professor Claudio Veliz, the *Australian* reported his speech uncritically, including his remark that in comparison with the brutality of the wars against the indigenous people waged by the Spaniards in Latin America the destruction of Aboriginal society had been like a "nun's picnic." The *Australian* reported a quotation in one of the books by Henry Reynolds that had been badly mangled, a point Reynolds readily conceded. The *Australian* (and not only it) pursued the claims Windschuttle made against Lyndall Ryan with partisan ferocity. Lane approached the vice chancellor of Ryan's university and her publisher, Allen & Unwin, asking them whether they intended to take action against their employee and their author. It turned out they did not, although posing the question undoubtedly affected her reputation.

The *Australian* had clearly made a decision to host a protracted debate on the worth of *Fabrication*. In the year following its publication, opinion columns and reviews were published on both sides of the debate in roughly equal number – on the one side Keith Windschuttle (on three occasions), Roger Sandall, Peter Ryan, Geoffrey Blainey, Frank Devine (twice), Peter Coleman and Janet Albrechtsen; on the other, Henry Reynolds, Lyndall Ryan, Bain Attwood, Dirk Moses, Stephen Foster, Martin Krygier with Robert van Krieken, and James Boyce.

By this time the *Australian*'s own position on the Windschuttle controversy it had provoked was clear. *Fabrication* was in its opinion a highly significant work of history which had mounted a formidable challenge to the idea of colonial genocide in the foundation of Australia. As such, it had acted as a much-needed corrective to the exaggerated black-armband view of Australian history. In addition it had exposed the slovenly standards and the left-wing bias of humanities scholars in Australian universities. The *Australian* published a letter signed by Stephen Muecke, Marcia Langton and Heather Goodall, which expressed regret about the willingness of the *Australian* to foster a debate on so reactionary a book. In their typical "censorious" fashion, the *Australian* argued, left-wing academics were trying to close down significant national debates. According to the editorial line of the *Australian*, if *Fabrication* had a fault, it was mainly one of "tone" – a failure to recognise that there was a tragic dimension in the destruction of the Tasmanian Aborigines.

Although the *Australian* had invited serious historical rejoinders to the questions raised by *Fabrication*, as soon as *Whitewash*, a critical anthology I had edited, was published, the project was characterised as the raising of a "posse" in an ad hominem bid to silence dissent. "The response of the academic establishment to Windschuttle's work," the *Australian* editorialised, "has been lamentable. It is supposed to be right-wing columnists who 'hunt in packs' but left-wing academics have done themselves proud with *Whitewash* in which 19 of them launch into Windschuttle's supposed failings as a historian and a human being."

The role of the *Australian* in the creation of the Windschuttle debate can be demonstrated in the following way. Following *Fabrication*, Windschuttle published two further books: the first a revisionist history trying to prove that the White Australia policy did not involve racism, the second trying to demonstrate that the idea of the stolen generations was a myth. Because the *Australian* did not endorse them, both had minimal impact on the national imagination and the national debate. Yet because of its editorial enthusiasm for *Fabrication*, within a year of the book's publication the *Australian* had turned Keith Windschuttle into a figure of national significance. Conservative Australians, including both John Howard and Tony Abbott, now embraced Windschuttle's fundamental conclusion, namely that the injustice of the indigenous dispossession had been wildly exaggerated by left-wing academics. In recognition of his significance as a cultural warrior, Howard appointed Windschuttle to the board of the ABC. Windschuttle understood what he owed to the *Australian*. At the launch of *Fabrication* he expressed surprise and gratitude at the early reception of his book by the press. And in a speech to a *Quadrant* gathering in 2007 he spoke of "Chris Mitchell's elevation to the editorship of the *Australian*" as one of the turning points in the Australian culture war, or as he put it, "one of the milestones in the process" whereby "a whole range of issues that had previously been taboo in mainstream publishing got an airing at last."

In an interview with me, Chris Mitchell claimed his personal relations with Windschuttle were remote and that his paper could not have maintained a prolonged debate about *Fabrication* or indeed any other topic in a social vacuum. Perhaps not. But the *Australian* had encouraged a debate about a book which had spoken of the kindness of the colonisers responsible for the deaths of almost all the Tasmanian Aborigines in the space of three decades, and which had characterised the victims as common criminals and as the agents of their own demise. *Fabrication* represented a kind of malign landmark in the intellectual history of Australia – a moment when the hard-won achievement of the generation of historians who built on the achievement of W.E.H. Stanner, C.D. Rowley and Henry

Reynolds in opening eyes to the tragedy of the Aboriginal dispossession was called into question. Because of the decision taken by the *Australian* to host the Windschuttle debate, the character of the nation was subtly but significantly changed.

It would be quite wrong to claim that the making of Keith Windschuttle was the only or even the primary contribution made by the *Australian* to the indigenous debate under Chris Mitchell. Under his editorship the *Australian* was responsible for two positive achievements. In particular through the reports of Tony Koch, Nicolas Rothwell and Paul Toohey, in their very different styles, the *Australian* has played a vital role in alerting the general public to the breakdown of conditions of life in the remote Aboriginal communities not only in the Northern Territory but across the country. In interview, Paul Kelly thought this was perhaps Mitchell's greatest contribution as editor-in-chief. Very many people would agree with him. The paper has also provided one of the most intellectually courageous Aboriginal leaders of contemporary times, Noel Pearson, with a permanent forum for the expression of his views.

Yet even here there have been great problems with the *Australian*'s coverage of indigenous affairs. By allowing Noel Pearson or those who agreed with him to become the sole interpreters of the breakdown within the remote indigenous communities, the paper adopted a position of what could be called univocalism. In the opinion pages there has been a near-complete absence of contrasting indigenous voices. Pearson is not the only indigenous intellectual. His views need to be tested and challenged. But there is more to it than this. Everyone involved with the indigenous community knows that opposition to Noel Pearson is very widespread. In a newspaper that has placed such an emphasis on indigenous affairs, the neglect of such voices itself represents a kind of distortion. As I will explain later in this essay, it seems likely that there are more indigenous people living under the federal Intervention in the Northern Territory that are opposed to it than are supportive. We might understand this better if oppositional indigenous voices, like those of Pat and Mick Dodson or

Larissa Behrendt, had been balanced against those of Pearson and his close ally, Marcia Langton. The *Australian*'s univocalism has seriously misled its readers about the balance of indigenous sentiment in the Northern Territory and elsewhere.

In addition, and even more obviously, the value of the attention the *Australian* paid to indigenous affairs was sullied by the role it played in the making of Keith Windschuttle. The widespread embrace by conservative Australians of Windschuttle's argument that the Tasmanian Aborigines were destroyed because they were an impossibly primitive people with a dysfunctional way of life helped to revive an even older tradition of Australian thought and sensibility: the straightforward denigration of Aboriginal culture. Without the support of the *Australian* the influence of Windschuttle would probably have been restricted to the ageing conservatives of the *Quadrant* circle. And without the influence of the Windschuttle debate on national sensibility, the following passage from another contributor to the *Australian*, Gary Johns of the Bennelong Society, would have almost certainly caused outrage of the kind that greeted Henry Bosch when in 1993 he spoke, far less chillingly, of Aborigines as a Stone Age people.

> Aborigines have had a hard time of it, or so the story goes ... [S]ome Aborigines have wanted both the whiteman's gifts and that which is inconsistent with living in the whiteman's world ... These are Aborigines and their white advisers who want to preserve Aboriginal culture. They deny that aspects of Aboriginal culture are totally inconsistent with basic human decency in its resort to violence and in its appalling treatment of women ... The false hope of the "other" world where the noble savage roamed is dead and buried, and for good reason.

In the *Australian* in 2006, Noel Pearson warned about the influence of Keith Windschuttle and Gary Johns:

I am very concerned about the damage conservative Australians are doing to the prospects of reconciliation through their uncritical endorsement of people like Keith Windschuttle and [Gary] Johns. The influence of Windschuttle and Johns has been such as to diminish public empathy with Aboriginal Australians ... Windschuttle's thesis about the absence of a notion of land ownership in Aboriginal Australia, and John's notion that our culture is unable to change and must therefore be left to die, are threatening the prospects of successful cooperation between Aboriginal Australians and conservatives.

Noel Pearson understands the dire implication for the very survival of his people if the Keith Windschuttle/Gary Johns viewpoint gains hold in Australia, as it now threatens to do, especially among conservatives. The same cannot be said for Chris Mitchell, the man who to his credit gave Pearson his national voice but was also crucial in the making of Keith Windschuttle, the writer and editor most responsible for the return of old racial attitudes which the nation, since the time of Stanner and Rowley, had struggled to transcend.

THE IRAQ INVASION: "AN OPEN AND SHUT CASE"

An alliance of neoconservatives and right-wing nationalists formed during the Clinton presidency. They were appointed to several key strategic positions inside the George W. Bush administration by Vice President Dick Cheney. Following the terrorist atrocity of September 11, this group began to drive the United States towards war with Iraq. About all this there was something exceedingly strange. September 11 was exclusively the work of al-Qaeda, which was based in Afghanistan. Iraq was not involved. To decide to attack Iraq following 9/11 was, as the American security chief Richard A. Clarke once observed, like deciding to attack Mexico as a reprisal for Pearl Harbor.

The key facts concerning Iraq were these. After Iraq invaded and occupied Kuwait in 1990, a US-led United Nations force drove it out. At this time Iraq possessed biological and chemical weapons, so-called weapons of mass destruction (WMD). Between 1991 and 1998 UN weapons inspectors were involved in the process of discovering and destroying Iraq's WMD arsenal. When, following political conflict, the inspectors left in 1998, parts of the arsenal remained unaccounted for. Following 9/11 the Cheney group in the Pentagon and the state department succeeded in convincing the president to invade Iraq. The argument of the war party in Washington went like this. Saddam Hussein already possessed chemical and biological weapons. He was certain to succeed in building nuclear weapons soon. Saddam was not merely a vicious tyrant. He led a regime that was officially described as a "rogue state." Rogue-state leaders such as Saddam were so irrational that they could not be "contained" by the threat of superior force in the way all Soviet leaders from Stalin to Brezhnev had been during the Cold War. Rather, Saddam was likely to use his WMD either directly, by waging war on Israel or Kuwait and then holding the world to ransom, or indirectly, by handing such weapons to al-Qaeda or a similar terrorist movement which might then mount a surprise 9/11-style attack on the United States or one of its allies. In either case, before the attacks there would be no warning. For this reason the United States was obliged to mount what was called a pre-emptive strike but which was in reality a preventive war, something which even the most hawkish US strategists at the height of the Cold War regarded as "unthinkable" and "repugnant."

In March 2003 the United States, along with forty-eight countries including the United Kingdom and Australia, waged a preventive war without the support of the UN Security Council. Following the invasion, hundreds of thousands of innocent men, women and children lost their lives and millions were displaced. As it turned out, the base claim of the Washington war party was false. Iraq possessed no WMD. The string of questionable, indeed highly implausible, assumptions about Saddam Hussein's likely behaviour, which was used to justify waging war, thus fell to the ground. The Iraq War is one of the greatest tragedies and scandals of contemporary history.

Rupert Murdoch was so close to the war leaders that in the days before the invasion, Tony Blair telephoned him on three occasions. Nor was his support merely personal. After the invasion Roy Greenslade of the *Guardian* investigated the editorial line of all 175 Murdoch newspapers around the globe. He found that each one had supported the invasion. This was not merely a question of editors intuitively grasping their owner's will. As I discovered during a trip to Tasmania after the invasion, for a brief time in 2002 one of Murdoch's papers, the *Hobart Mercury*, wrote anti-war editorials. It toed the Murdoch line only after a warning letter came from News Limited's Australian head office. Nor did Murdoch bother to disguise his determination to mobilise his media empire on behalf of the Iraq War. On 18 February 2003, he told the *Bulletin*: "We can't back down now, where you hand over the whole of the Middle East to Saddam … I think Bush is acting very morally, very correctly, and I think he is going to go on with it." Eighteen months later, in his typical lapidary manner, Murdoch informed an ABC journalist, "With our newspapers we have indeed supported Bush's foreign policy. And we remain committed that way."

The *Australian* is Murdoch's most important vehicle for influencing Australian politics. It is unthinkable that it could have been anti-war. Given all this, even if an enthusiastic neoconservative like Chris Mitchell had not been appointed editor-in-chief during the build-up to war, the *Australian* would have supported the Iraq invasion. On this question, Murdoch's newspapers did not exercise autonomy.

I must add a significant caveat here. At the time of the invasion of Iraq the editor of the opinion pages was Tom Switzer, a disciple of Owen Harries, the Australian editor of the US journal the *National Interest* and a conservative foreign-policy realist. Switzer was opposed to the invasion. According to his count, between July 2002 and March 2003 the *Australian* ran "45 dovish ... and 47 hawkish" opinion columns. Although in my review this undercounts the explicitly and implicitly pro-war pieces by at least twenty, it is still true that before the invasion the only reasonably balanced section of the paper was the opinion page. Everywhere else the paper overwhelmingly supported it. This was the reason why, in March 2006, John Howard said that Chris Mitchell's *Australian* had been "a very strong supporter of our military operations in Iraq."

However, it is not so much the fact of that support but its tone that is significant and revealing. These qualities are best demonstrated by a study of the Mitchell-inspired editorials and the commentaries of the *Australian*'s foreign editor, Greg Sheridan.

Throughout the build-up to war the *Australian*'s leader articles and the Sheridan commentaries supported without question every aspect of the official line of the Washington war party. The evidence was incontrovertible that Iraq presently possessed chemical and biological WMD and was very close to possessing nuclear weapons. Saddam Hussein did indeed pose a danger to the world in our era of a kind similar to the threat of Hitler in the 1930s. As a consequence it was gravest folly to "appease" him. It might have been "noble" for the Americans and the British to try to win the support of the UN Security Council before the invasion, but from the legal and political point of view that was unnecessary. There was indeed a very real danger that Saddam Hussein might suddenly invade Kuwait or launch an unprovoked attack on Israel. There was an equally real danger that he might hand his WMD to al-Qaeda or a similar terrorist group. Even though the new US strategic doctrine of the pre-emptive strike, which justified waging war on the basis of an imagined future threat, clearly represented a revolution in international law, it was supported in the *Australian*'s leaders and the Sheridan pre-war commentaries as if it was altogether unremarkable and the merest common sense.

Every part of this case was wrong or dangerous. Yet the errors of judgment were not the most damaging dimension of the *Australian*'s editorial argument for the invasion of Iraq. More damaging was the attempt to create an atmosphere where cautious considerations of facts and arguments were seen as examples of stupidity, or as the betrayal of the national interest, or as ideological blindness. Examination of one pre-war Sheridan commentary and one Mitchell-inspired leader is the best way to reveal the overweeningly self-confident, uncritical, unreflective and bullying style because of which – on the question of the invasion of Iraq and so many other critical international and national questions over the past ten years – the possibility of a sober national debate was made more difficult.

In September 2002 Tony Blair released his government's dossier on Iraq's WMD. As it happens, everything contained in it turned out to be entirely false. But that is not my point. Upon its release no one outside the intelligence world, and perhaps few inside it, was in any position to judge its accuracy. The task of journalists was to inform citizens of its content and to pose critical questions about the potential problems of this kind of intelligence information. Here, however, is what Sheridan wrote.

"The Blair dossier should transform the debate over the Iraq threat. Either Tony Blair is a monstrous liar or Saddam Hussein is. Take your pick." The dossier was "telling and sober." Hussein had "never at any stage since the Gulf War … given up his program to acquire WMDs." Presently he possessed "substantial biological and chemical weapons that could be deployed within 45 minutes." He was also "continuing his nuclear weapons programs apace" and was "one or two years away from producing nuclear weapons." Saddam Hussein had learned from previous experience how to hide his weapons from inspectors. Accordingly their return would most likely be valueless. Sheridan's "inescapable conclusion" was that "inspections are not workable." The only way war could be avoided now was for Saddam Hussein to reveal his weapons and destroy them in full public view. "Anything less and he is, as usual, just jerking the UN's chain, all the while moving closer to his goal of nuclear dominance of the Middle East."

This was not an analysis of the Blair dossier. Not only did Sheridan take every claim made by Blair on trust. Not only did he pose no critical questions about the dossier. Implicitly, by asking readers to choose whether it was Tony Blair or Saddam Hussein who was a "monstrous liar," he treated anyone with doubts about WMD as a conscious or unconscious dupe of the dictator. Moreover Sheridan outbid even the formal case of the war party in Washington. For him the total cooperation of the Saddam Hussein regime in the weapons inspection process was insufficient. So certain was he that Saddam possessed a vast WMD arsenal, so convinced was he of the capacity of Saddam to deceive the UN weapons inspectors, that the only means by which Saddam could avoid war was to destroy his arsenal himself. What Sheridan's logic entailed was that if Iraq had no WMD to destroy, it had to be invaded. In this article Sheridan mocked the arguments of the anti-war Labor Left as "the shrill and politically semi-literate anti-Americanism of those hitherto hidden Metternichs." In another article of this time he suggested that anyone who thought that Saddam Hussein might be telling the truth about his WMD was in need of immediate psychiatric assistance. Throughout the period leading to the invasion of Iraq, Sheridan did not write reports or analysis. With considerable rhetorical skill, with an entire absence of self-doubt, with a total contempt for those with whom he disagreed and a fawning infatuation with those Americans of the war party, like Paul Wolfowitz or Rich Armitage, who granted him interviews – he used his journalism for one purpose only, to beat the drum of war.

In late November 2002 UN weapons inspectors led by Hans Blix returned to Iraq. On 27 January 2003, Blix reported on the progress of his team, UNMOVIC, to the Security Council. It was a tough and critical but also balanced and nuanced account. Iraq had "on the whole cooperated rather well" in the inspection process. Certain documents he asked for had been provided; others had not yet been. Certain personnel had been interviewed, but not enough of them and only with officials present. Even though much biological agent had been destroyed in the past, Blix was still worried that while Iraq claimed that it had destroyed all its biological agents, it had not yet provided UNMOVIC with the proof. A 12,000-page document of December 2002 regrettably largely comprised old material, but there was some important new material in it as well. And so on. In retrospect, as Blix argued in his memoir, he did not disagree with the analysis of a journalist he respected that his tough report sought to convince Baghdad to save itself by becoming more helpful, more quickly. His general attitude was this: "UNMOVIC ... is not presuming that there are proscribed items and activities in Iraq, but nor is it ... presuming the opposite."

On 29 January 2003, the *Australian* editorialised on the Blix report which it called, altogether fancifully and fictitiously, "a chronicle of despair." The editorial is a good illustration of its ferocious pursuit of war and its willingness to bend the truth to suit its purpose. The *Australian* claimed that Blix's report was "an inventory of a shop of horrors" and that "the evidence that this regime is committed to arming itself with weapons of a horror that equals and even exceeds nuclear warheads is incontrovertible." Blix had in fact argued clearly, as we have seen, that the existence of WMD in Iraq could, at this stage of the inspections, neither be presumed nor denied. While admitting sotto voce that inspectors were allowed to visit "specific sites as requested," the *Australian* claimed that the Blix report "details how the Iraqis are cooperating with the UN team in form rather than substance and that they confect excuses to make the inspectors' work as difficult as possible. Saddam's regime dances the dance of cooperation, but slowly and clumsily and with a desire to lead their partner away from the regime's laboratories and weapons dumps." This is a near-complete distortion. Blix argued that "Iraq has on the whole cooperated rather well so far with UNMOVIC in this field ... access has been provided to all sites ... and with one exception it has been prompt. We have further had great help in building up the infrastructure of our office in Baghdad ..." He hoped that the excellent cooperation in "process" would soon be equalled in "substance," that is to say by the regime's voluntarily surrendering any existing WMD items or providing incontrovertible proof of their destruction. Blix had tried to explain what he meant about cooperation in substance by arguing that in comparison with the South African process of nuclear disarmament, "Iraq appears not to have come to a genuine acceptance – not even today – of the disarmament, which was demanded of it ..." The *Australian* pounced, as did the supporters of war in Washington and London. "This sentence alone," the *Australian* argued, "justified military action." In his memoir Blix reflected ruefully about how the Washington war party had made great mischief with these words.

For the *Australian* the moral of the Blix report was clear. Saddam had retained a WMD arsenal. It was certain that "sooner or later he would use them" against Israel or Kuwait as he once had against the Kurds. Sanctions against Saddam Hussein would not work. Nor could a case now be made for delay. Saddam was a master of "delay and obfuscation." While the will of the United States was strong, the will of the United Nations was notoriously weak. The Security Council must make up its mind quickly. If Blix wanted to continue with the apparently futile inspections, he must be given a firm date in the near future before reporting back to the UN. If his report remained unsatisfactory, it would be time for military action. If the UN failed in its duty, the United States and its allies must "serve the world community by taking on the burden alone." In this entirely typical pre-war editorial, the spirit of the Blix report had been thoroughly misrepresented by the *Australian* in order to advance the case for war. In the same edition of the paper, the full text of Blix's UN speech was published. If anyone actually read it, they would have been amazed.

On the eve of war, the front-page headlines of the *Australian* began to appear in capitals. War came. Headlines were now not only capitalised but doubled in size. **FIRST STRIKE ON BAGHDAD. PUNCH INTO IRAQ**. Within three weeks, because of its overwhelmingly superior force, the "Coalition of the Willing" had reached Baghdad. Huge bold capitalised headlines captured the Murdoch empire's political message. **REGIME IN RUINS. SADDAM'S GRAVE? END OF A TYRANT. TYRANTS BEWARE**. On 11 and 12 April, the *Australian* supported this atmosphere with two triumphalist editorials. The first located the victory within the neo-conservative post–Cold War narrative. The collapse of the regime of Saddam Hussein in 2003 was the Middle-Eastern equivalent of the fall of the Berlin Wall in 1989. Once again the people were dancing in the streets. The thirst for freedom was universal and unquenchable. The second editorial drew the domestic implications of the victory for what it called the "culture war fought within the West." While "the performance of the mainstream Left" had been "politically inept," the performance of the self-hating anti-Western "intellectual Left" had been nothing less than "a disgrace." A "fascinating case" in this regard was Carmen Lawrence, who had predicted that as a result of the war there might be "three million refugees" and that "nearly half-a-million Iraqis would be killed." As the editorial sneered, this was "wrong but only by a factor of 400." "Never underestimate the power of ideology and myth – in this case anti-Americanism – to trump reality. But at least we know for sure it is not love, but being a left-wing intellectual, that means never having to say you're sorry."

This breezy editorial was in part penned by the *Australian*'s resident right-wing intellectual smart-aleck, Imre Salusinszky. It was entitled: "Coalition of the Whining Got it Wrong." Re-reading this editorial was a strange experience. Since the invasion of Iraq there have been more than three million refugees and another 1.5 million internally displaced people. The most plausible figure for civilian deaths due to the invasion is, in my view, between 300,000 and 400,000.

It was typical of the mentality of the intellectual Left, the *Australian* argued in an editorial on 11 April 2003, that already there were complaints that no weapons of mass destruction – the *casus belli* justifying the invasion – had been discovered. It called for patience. As weeks and then months passed, and as the fearful disorder that the invasion had visited upon Iraq was beginning to become clear, it dawned on the advocates of war at the *Australian* that the non-discovery of WMD posed an awkward problem. How they responded to the non-appearance of WMD was a useful way of assessing their capacity for self-criticism and their political character.

Sheridan simply could not admit to himself that he had been wrong, or to put it in his foolish language, that it had been Tony Blair and not Saddam Hussein who had been the "monstrous liar." On 10 July 2003, he published an article, "WMD Doubts are Ludicrous," in which he claimed that the hard-line state department right-winger John Bolton had provided him "almost as an afterthought" with the "sensational" evidence that would prove the existence of Saddam's WMD arsenal. "The evidence that Hussein had WMD programs is so overwhelming [Bolton] can barely understand how it is doubted." The evidence never appeared. On 31 January 2004, in a Basil Fawlty–like performance, Sheridan sought to explain the apparent absence of WMD. Was it not possible that Saddam's denials were deliberately unconvincing, attempts to fool his neighbours that he still possessed them without providing the West with a smoking gun? Or again, perhaps his own scientists had misled Saddam into believing that Iraq did indeed possess WMD. "It is a bit much to expect the CIA to know more about the internal situation in Iraq than Hussein himself." In his heart of hearts, Sheridan was still not convinced. Even after the Washington hawk David Kay, who had been put onto the case by George W. Bush, concluded that Iraq had not possessed a WMD arsenal for several years, Sheridan thought it perfectly possible that stockpiles "are buried and as yet unfound, or that they were transported to Syria." In late February 2004 he spoke of these matters to two retired Israeli intelligence experts. They expressed the opinion that "two living rooms full of key biological and chemical material" might yet be discovered. Sheridan thought this "plausible." Of one thing, however, he was sure. In a coming parliamentary inquiry into the Australian intelligence failure over Iraq, John Howard "should not make any admissions of error by his Government or the intelligence services. To do so would be wrong in fact and would tend to demoralise his supporters."

One of the greatest weaknesses of Chris Mitchell's editorship of the *Australian* is that he has allowed Greg Sheridan to remain his foreign editor throughout. Sheridan is a man who argued in different columns that George W. Bush was the Winston Churchill of our era; that unlike mediocre politicians like Barack Obama and John McCain, the "new star" of American politics, Sarah Palin, was able to combine "celebrity" with "character"; that President Obama's "anti-Israel hysteria" was leading his administration toward "licensing a mutant strain of anti-semitism"; and that the United States would most likely be strengthened by the crash of Wall Street in September 2008. Throughout the Mitchell years Sheridan has displayed almost no interest in either global poverty or climate change. A Factiva data search brings up one passing reference to the UN's Millennium Development Goals. In one of his columns, he based his climate change denialism on the rising house prices at Vaucluse. The problem with Sheridan is not that he lacks eloquence or intelligence or even that he is so right-wing. The problem is that he lacks judgment and the capacity to learn from his many, many egregious mistakes.

The *Australian's* editorial response to the absence of a WMD arsenal was even more revealing than that of its foreign editor. On 7 June 2003, the *Australian* posed the fundamental question: "Where are Iraq's weapons of mass destruction?" As the governments of the US and UK had assured the world of "the horrors of Saddam's armoury," they should now either "produce evidence the weapons existed or explain why they cannot." It argued that although WMD might never be discovered, the evidence for their existence at the time of the invasion was "overwhelming." Perhaps Saddam had "dispersed" his weapons. Perhaps he had "destroyed the evidence." In any case, although it was admittedly taking too long to restore order in Iraq, because of the "quick and relatively bloodless victory" the benefits were already flowing. A tyrant had been toppled. The possibility for a lasting peace settlement between the Israelis and Palestinians had been created.

In December 2003 Saddam Hussein was captured. On 20 December the *Australian* published a very upbeat editorial. The people were jubilant. Bazaars were opening. A free press existed. The paper was now willing to accept that WMD might not have existed when Iraq was invaded. "It now appears that much of the intelligence allied governments relied on was wrong." However, Saddam's track record as a "warmonger" and the *Australian*'s self-generated supposed fact that "he refused to cooperate with the United Nations team led by Hans Blix" meant that Saddam was "the architect of his own doom." I had once assumed that the idea that war was to be regarded as a last resort was a consensual Western value. Not apparently at the *Australian*. It argued that "when national security is involved, erring on the side of caution is no crime." According to this logic, it was better to go to war – even if that risked massive loss of life and the creation of decades of disorder for a non-Western people – than to endure the possibility of a new terrorist attack on a Western country.

On 20 March 2004, the anniversary of the invasion, the *Australian* published another editorial, "We were right to go to war against Iraq." It acknowledged that "Western intelligence monstrously misjudged the extent of Saddam's existing arsenal." It argued that "there is no such thing as a good war." But it also argued that some wars are self-evidently "just" and must therefore be fought and that Iraq was a clear example. The Coalition of the Willing had gone to war not only on the basis of false intelligence, but also a set of wildly implausible assumptions about the future behaviour of Iraq and a strategic doctrine that would overturn any civilised conception of international law. And yet, in the words of the

Australian, the question of whether the war on Iraq was just, unbelievably enough, was "an open and shut case."

That war was responsible for the deaths of up to 400,000 people and the displacement of millions more. And yet Chris Mitchell's *Australian* has not expressed one word of remorse or explanation for the enthusiastic and uncritical support it had given to the war. Apparently it is not being a left-wing intellectual but an editor-in-chief of the *Australian* that means never having to say you're sorry.

MEDIA WATCH: "THEY ARE CERTAINLY NOT GOOD ENOUGH TO JUDGE US"

When observing the behaviour of the chess champion Bobby Fischer, Arthur Koestler coined a very useful neologism: "mimophant." "A mimophant," he wrote, "is a hybrid species: a cross between a mimosa and an elephant. A member of this species is sensitive like a mimosa where his own feelings are concerned and thick-skinned like an elephant trampling over the feelings of others." In contemporary Australia the most significant example of this is the editorial team at the *Australian*. The mimophancy of the *Australian* is best illustrated by the strange story of its protracted feud with the ABC program *Media Watch*.

From the mid-1990s a new kind of columnist – right-wing attack dogs, I call them – emerged in the Australian mainstream press. Such journalists were closely associated with the Howard government and the culture of populist conservatism it fostered. The *Sydney Morning Herald* had Miranda Devine and Paul Sheehan, the *Daily Telegraph* Piers Akerman and Tim Blair, the *Herald Sun* Andrew Bolt and the *Australian* Frank Devine, Christopher Pearson and Janet Albrechtsen.

After *Tampa* and 9/11 the group turned its attention to "the Muslim problem." No one did so more insistently or stridently than Janet Albrechtsen. On 17 July 2002, following the conviction of two Muslim brothers who had raped a young "Australian" woman, she wrote about the phenomenon of what the French call "*tournantes*" – "take your turn" – "the pack rape of white girls by young Muslim men." For evidence of this practice, Albrechtsen relied in part on the witness of two European professors, Jean-Jacques Rassial of Villetaneuse University and Flemming Balvig of Copenhagen University. Albrechtsen characterised such behaviour as common among a minority of youthful Muslim males. She argued that the failure of liberal-minded multiculturalists to confront this problem "head on" would play into the hands of the next Pauline Hanson.

Media Watch is a fifteen-minute program that screens on ABC television on Monday nights. In 2002 David Marr was the presenter, on leave from his employer the *Sydney Morning Herald*. By any reasonably objective standards Marr was (and is) one of Australia's most distinguished journalists, author of the superb biography of Patrick White and co-author of the most important history of the Howard government's asylum-seeker policy, *Dark Victory*. Marr is also indubitably a man of the Left.

On 9 September Marr examined the lamentable performance of the media in reporting on what he described as "perhaps the worst series of rapes Sydney has ever seen." Marr's primary target was Alan Jones, who was at the time running a campaign to undermine the police commissioner, Peter Ryan. Towards the end of the segment Marr turned his attention to Janet Albrechtsen. In her column of 17 July, Marr argued, Albrechtsen appeared to have "lifted" a sentence from an article by Adam Sage in the *Times* of 5 December 2000. Albrechtsen had argued: "French and Danish experts say perpetrators of gang rape flounder between their parents' Islamic values and society's more liberal democratic values, falling back on the most basic pack mentality of violence and self-gratification." The *Times'* article had claimed: "Caught between their parents' Islamic values and society's Christian and social democratic values, some youths appear to have fallen back on the most basic instincts of violence and pleasure."

But Albrechtsen was guilty not merely of plagiarism, Marr went on to note. When contacted by *Media Watch*, the Danish expert she had cited, Professor Balvig, said: "The citation is completely wrong. What I have said is, that the main explanation of gang rape probably is social, and not religious or cultural." Even worse, however, Albrechtsen had clearly doctored the *Times'* passage reporting the views of the other professor, Jean-Jacques Rassial. Rassial was paraphrased in the *Times* as saying that "gang rape had become an initiation rite for male adolescents in city suburbs." By inserting the word "white" before girls and the word "Muslim" before youth, Albrechtsen had turned this into "Pack rape of white girls is an initiation rite of passage for a small section of young male

Muslim youth, said Jean-Jacques Rassial, a psychotherapist at Villetaneuse University." When contacted by Media Watch, Rassial was outraged by what he took to be Albrechtsen's deliberate distortion of his views: "In France today, one would not describe this situation using terms like 'blanches' (white women) or 'musulmans' (muslims); and, none other than extremists from the Far Right would dream of using the labels 'européenes' (European women) and 'mahgrébins' (north Africans) ... There would be grounds, in France, to insist on a correction, even sue for defamation ..."

Janet Albrechtsen's misdemeanours in her column were truly "an open and shut case." Much later, at the end of 2002, Marr called for the Australian to sack Albrechtsen. This was perhaps an overreaction. But what seems clear, at least to me, was that, given the self-evident wrongdoing in this case, a mature journalist and a mature newspaper would have, in the great Australian colloquialism, "copped it sweet." This was not the response of the Australian. Marr's segment precipitated nothing less than a two-and-a-half-year vendetta against him, and a five-year vendetta against Media Watch, which became in the Australian's eyes the symbol of the pernicious left-wing culture that still controlled the ABC. There is space here only for its most significant or most startling or most absurd moments.

On 18 September 2002, Janet Albrechtsen launched a furious retaliatory strike against David Marr. She revealed that she had been interviewed for the post of Media Watch presenter but had been rejected because – shock, horror – she had confessed to being the kind of political animal banned from the ABC, namely a conservative. (The interviewer, the ABC's Simon West, soon denied the charge in a letter to the editor. Marr informed me she was in fact rejected as a possible right-wing co-host because her audition performance had been "so wooden.") Who then got the gig? None other than David Marr, the notorious left-winger. Under his regime Media Watch censored opinion and closed down debate. Even worse, taxpayers were supporting the prosecution of his notorious feuds against Alan Jones and Paul Sheehan. Media Watch never criticised left-wingers. It shamelessly pursued Marr's anti-Howard and anti-Murdoch agendas. In allowing Marr free rein, once again the ABC board had miserably failed to do its duty. There should be a public inquiry. "This public asset has been hijacked." Strangely enough, there was not one word in Albrechtsen's column about the charges Marr had laid about plagiarism and misquotation.

On 6 November 2003, the *Australian* revived the Albrechtsen issue. In its Media section, the editor Michael Stutchbury provided a 2300-word summary of the case against Marr marshalled by Paul Sheehan in his weird new book *The Electronic Whorehouse*. Sheehan and Stutchbury implicitly blamed Marr for all the unkind words that had been uttered about Albrechtsen since the *Media Watch* segment. Both suggested that her plagiarism and misquotations were forgivable because on the issue of substance – the intolerable behaviour of young Muslim males and the gutlessness in response to it of those she called Multicultural Man – she was both courageous and right. A prime example of Multicultural Man was one of her victims, Professor Rassial. As a typical Multicultural Man, Rassial admitted that he had not been willing to examine rape from the ethnic or religious point of view. Apparently, then, there should have been no great fuss about Albrechtsen inventing quotes about what he should have said. On the same day the *Australian* published an editorial in part about the Albrechtsen–Marr Affair. It conceded that *Media Watch* "had found a chink in Albrechtsen's armour when she incorrectly ascribed a particular view to a couple of European professors." But so what? This trivial mistake had been "prized and twisted" until it had turned "into a floodgate of abusive personalised attacks." The purpose was, as always with the Left, to close down much-needed debate. "It is as though Marr's *Media Watch* was determined to prove – to embody – the case against the ABC." The *Australian* had advertised the Stutchbury–Sheehan story with an illustration showing Janet Albrechtsen as the victim of left-wing media "pack rape." This was too much even for the *Australian's* own journalists. Sixty signed a letter to the editor calling the use of the term in this context "offensive and inappropriate." The letter was not published in the *Australian*. It did, however, find its way onto the *Media Watch* website.

David Marr left his post at the end of 2004. The editorial writers at the *Australian* celebrated his retirement by claiming that Marr had "weakened" the *Media Watch* "brand." Unlike the *Australian*, which did not support either "side of politics," Marr had "subordinated a rational assessment of the media's weaknesses to his obsession with the perfidy of Howard, Bush and Blair." The *Australian* used the occasion to claim that in a recent lecture delivered to the "loopy-Left little magazine" *Overland*, Marr "compares the ascendancy of John Howard to the rise of Hitler." This was an astonishing but unfortunately quite typical distortion. Marr had merely argued that he had come to agree with a point of view once expressed to him by a conservative Catholic, Senator Brian Harradine – illustrated by the electoral strength of the Nazi Party before Hitler came to power – that on many political issues popularity was an unreliable standard. The case Marr most had in mind was the strong support enjoyed by the Howard government's cruel asylum-seeker policy.

Shortly after Marr's retirement, as it happened, Janet Albrechtsen was appointed by the Howard government to the ABC Board. In cultural struggles of this kind it is certainly valuable to have friends in high places.

During the period between early 2005 and mid-2007, when Liz Jackson (2005) and Monica Attard (from the beginning of 2006) were the presenters of *Media Watch*, tensions occasionally flared between the program and the *Australian* but in general at a lower level of intensity than during the days of David Marr. In 2006 Mark Scott replaced Russell Balding as ABC managing director. Scott decided to try to appease right-wing critics of the ABC. Gerard Henderson had for years been one of the most relentless critics of ABC left-wing bias in general and of *Media Watch* in particular. In the felicitous words of a former *Media Watch* producer, David Salter, in a characteristic "blizzard of hairsplitting" he had recently engaged in a protracted email correspondence with the program's producer, Peter McEvoy, which took forty-four pages to print out. In October, Scott chose the headquarters of Gerard Henderson's Sydney Institute to make the cultural concession the Right had long awaited: "I suspect that we are by no means as bad as our critics might suggest and not as blameless as our defenders might wish." Scott even singled out *Media Watch* for criticism. He told his audience that he "had encouraged the director of television [Kim Dalton] to work with the *Media Watch* team to review their format and content next year to ensure there is more opportunity for debate and discussion around contentious and important issues." He also introduced new general anti-bias guidelines and structures. The *Australian* reported that it was Janet Albrechtsen who "initiated the changes."

During the first half of 2007, under its feisty but rather determinedly non-ideological presenter, Monica Attard, and her new producer, Tim Palmer, *Media Watch* scarcely commented on the *Australian*. It appeared to me as if, in the long Indian arm-wrestle between the *Australian* and *Media Watch*, the *Australian* had won. This judgment underestimated the grit of Attard and Palmer.

On 20 August *Media Watch* took up a serious issue concerning the *Australian*. Eleven days earlier the paper had published a front-page story which claimed that the visiting head of the Intergovernmental Panel on Climate Change, Dr Rajendra Pachauri, had "backed the Howard Government's decision to defer setting a long-term target for reducing greenhouse emissions until the full facts are known." The story was written by the *Australian*'s environment writer, Matthew Warren, who had recently been hired after a period as a lobbyist for the New South Wales Minerals Council. It was given the headline "Climate expert backs Canberra." That evening Pachauri delivered a lecture in Sydney. He was asked why as head of the IPCC he had supported the Howard government's decision to defer the setting of a long-term emissions reduction target. He replied that he had done no such thing. "I got a telephone call from an important ambassador from Canberra this morning asking me how the devil did you make so and so a statement. And I said it comes as a surprise to me. I didn't say that. I've obviously been misquoted." Pachauri decided that he needed to publish a letter to the editor of the *Australian* correcting the record. On *Media Watch* Monica Attard read out a part of Pachauri's letter:

"I am writing to convey my deep disappointment at the news report in your newspaper … Nothing I said in my telephone interview with Mr Matthew Warren implied or even remotely conveyed that I supported or opposed the Australian Government's policies on climate change. I am surprised that a very general opinion that I expressed without reference to any country was twisted around to create the impression that I supported the current government's stance on climate change." Astonishingly, Attard pointed out, the *Australian* had refused to publish Pachauri's letter. Even more astonishingly, on 18 August, after receiving it, the *Weekend Australian* had published a story on the nuclear industry which claimed: "Rajendra Pachauri recently backed Canberra's decision to defer a long-term target for reducing greenhouse emissions …"

Can a newspaper suffer a brain snap? It seems that it can. In response to this coolly analytical but devastating *Media Watch* segment, on 23 August the *Australian* published no fewer than four long pieces purporting to show that it was innocent of all wrongdoing and that *Media Watch* was a disgrace. One of Chris Mitchell's go-to journalists at delicate moments of crisis was Caroline Overington. In an article in the media section, "Ripping yarns you won't be watching on the ABC," she inquired over 1660 words: what exactly is wrong with *Media Watch*? Why on Monday did it not analyse what she called "the Brissenden affair" – a recent controversy concerning an "off the record" conversation with Peter Costello two years earlier about his leadership ambitions which three Canberra press gallery journalists had revealed? Why did it not report on the recent Fairfax "fiasco," the claim that the wreck of HMAS *Sydney* had been discovered? Why did it not tell its viewers about the *Sydney Morning Herald*'s suppression of a vital story concerning Kevin Rudd's visit to a New York strip club? It was not until her ninth paragraph that Overington let readers into the secret of what her harangue was actually about. Confronted by an embarrassment of riches, Monday's program had in fact been full of "pointless items." She named them. "At the risk of being accused of withholding information … there was also what executive producer Tim Palmer described as 'an allegation' that this newspaper had 'misrepresented, possibly' the views of a climate change expert."

Caroline Overington's case was supported by a 1450-word editorial – "Old tricks back at *Media Watch*." Unlike Overington, the editorial was upfront about the issue in dispute. Despite Pachauri's misconceived views on the matter, he had not been misrepresented. He "should have known what he was doing." The implication here was interesting. As Pachauri was not qualified to judge whether or not he had been misrepresented, there was no reason to publish his letter. The editorial seethed with scarcely controlled rage and indignation. "Why bother with a media television program," it began, "that lacks journalistic integrity and conducts its affairs along the lines of an insiders' club that pushes its ideological prejudices at taxpayers' expense?" In the eyes of the editorial team at the *Australian*, the altogether unjustified attack by *Media Watch* was no accident. The anti–News Limited "institutional bias" of *Media Watch* went so deep that it might not even be aware of it itself. Even more, an insidious "political nexus" existed between "the ABC and Fairfax." "As a newspaper we welcome evaluation of our work but tire of having to continually engage with the malicious and increasingly irrational questioning" of *Media Watch*'s writers and producers. It was "a poor excuse for a program." If its "standards do not improve, the program should be scrapped." And, most revealingly of all for those with an interest in psychology, *Media Watch* was "certainly not good enough to judge us."

With this editorial the *Australian* had declared formal war on *Media Watch*. To use the language it had deployed in the case of David Marr and Janet Albrechtsen, it had found a "chink" in *Media Watch*'s armour – the failure on 20 August to analyse what the *Australian* called "the Brissenden affair" – and turned it into the occasion for "a floodgate of abusive personalised attacks." The *Australian* asked its regular contributing writer on *Media Watch*, the former producer David Salter, why the program had been so remiss. He leant towards a plausible "sinister" explanation. Because Brissenden was an ABC journalist, the program might have been unwilling to subject him "to the same level of ethical scrutiny it applies to others." The *Australian* sought the opinion of the managing director of the ABC, Mark Scott, on the revealing omission. Scott told a journalist at the *Australian*, Ean Higgins, "I was surprised not to see it on *Media Watch*. I was thinking they would cover it." Higgins pointed out that "Scott's emphasis on the seriousness of the controversy contrasts with the view *Media Watch* producer Tim Palmer expressed to *The Australian* … in which he said the story had been 'sucked dry.'" Soon the *Australian* sought the opinion of the prime minister on a matter of such grave national significance as the failure of *Media Watch* to analyse "the Brissenden affair." Caroline Overington reported that John Howard "thinks the ABC's *Media Watch* is an odd program because it does not cover major media stories of the day" like this one. By the time the opinion of the prime minister on the Brissenden affair had been solicited and published, both Tim Palmer and Monica Attard had announced their retirements from *Media Watch*. When Overington now contacted Palmer on an unrelated matter, according to her he uttered "an unprintable profanity to describe one journalist and called the editor 'an idiot.'"

The furious open warfare between the *Australian* and *Media Watch* continued until the program went into recess at the end of 2007. The *Australian* engaged in a series of pre-emptive strikes, attacking the program even before segments went to air for putting questions to its journalists. The chief battles occurred over the high-level Liberal Party connections of Janet Albrechtsen; a visit by Dennis Shanahan to Iraq; and, most violently of all, a story published in the *Weekend Australian* which revealed the names of two pregnant Northern Territory Aboriginal girls, one twelve years old, the other thirteen. Palmer and Attard went down all guns blazing. They even experienced a kind of death-bed revenge. Caroline Overington had been assigned the task of reporting the election contest between the Liberal Party's Malcolm Turnbull and the Labor Party's George Newhouse. One of the candidates was a former lover of Newhouse, climate change activist Danielle Ecuyer. Overington was so keen to see to whom Ecuyer's preferences would flow that she sent her an extraordinarily improper email: "Please preference Malcolm. It would be such a good front-page story. Also, he'd be a loss to the parliament and George – forgive me – would be no gain. :)" Ecuyer, outraged, took the story to *Media Watch*. Overington described her own behaviour as nothing but an obvious, good-natured joke. Newhouse took the opportunity to release emails Overington had sent him during the Wentworth campaign in which she had first propositioned and then threatened him. Chris Mitchell described Caroline Overington's Ecuyer email as "colourful." On election day, at a polling station, Overington approached Newhouse and struck him on the head. Shortly after, an enigmatic apology to Newhouse appeared in the *Australian*. Everything appeared to be spinning out of control.

CLIMATE CHANGE: "CLEAR, CATASTROPHIC THREATS"

When I was a schoolboy, part of the English syllabus was called "clear thinking." I hope some equivalent still is. For we have never been more in need of the capacity for clear thinking than we are with regard to the controversy over climate change that has raged, especially in the United States and Australia, over the past few years. The key facts and distinctions are so obvious that it is both embarrassing and dismaying that they need to be pointed out. But they do.

The first and most important fact is that there is a consensual view among qualified scientists about the cause of climate change. This consensus provided the basis for the four reports of the United Nations' Intergovernmental Panel on Climate Change, the most recent of which summarised the research of the 1500 or so leading climate scientists across the globe. Naomi Oreskes demonstrated the existence of this consensus by a straightforward method. She read the abstracts of 928 scientific papers connected to climate change that were published between 1993 and 2003 in the relevant peer-reviewed scientific journals. Her conclusion, published in *Science*, December 2004, was: "Remarkably, none of the papers disagreed with the consensus position." Climate change "sceptics" have, of course, made attempts to find fault with her research. They have failed. Perhaps the easiest way to demonstrate both the existence of the consensus and its core content is to reproduce the first part of a letter that was sent to every US Senator on 21 October 2009 by the American Association for the Advancement of Science on behalf of eighteen national scientific and mathematical associations representing the relevant climate-science disciplines:

> As you consider climate change legislation, we, as leaders of scientific organizations, write to state the consensus scientific view. Observations throughout the world make it clear that climate change is occurring, and rigorous scientific research demonstrates

that the greenhouse gases emitted by human activities are the primary driver. These conclusions are based on multiple independent lines of evidence, and contrary assertions are inconsistent with an objective assessment of the vast body of peer-reviewed science. Moreover there is strong evidence that ongoing climate change will have broad impacts on society, including the global economy and on the environment. For the United States, climate change impacts include sea level rise for coastal states, greater threats of extreme weather events, and increased risk of regional water scarcity, urban heat waves, western wildfires, and the disturbance of biological systems throughout the country.

On the question of the scientific consensus on climate change, the waters have been muddied by the failure to draw an obvious distinction. On the fundamental theory of the climate scientists – namely, that global warming is happening; that it is primarily caused by the emission of greenhouse gases, most importantly carbon dioxide; and that it is certain to have profound effects in the future – the science is truly settled. However, in regard to scores of other questions – concerning the precise impact increases in atmospheric carbon dioxide and other greenhouse gases will have on global temperature and the precise impact rising global temperature will have on sea levels, the acidification of the oceans, the rate of melting of the continental icesheets on Greenland and Antarctica or the Siberian permafrost or the Himalayan glaciers, the pace at which the extinction of different species will occur, the prevalence and intensity of hurricanes, wildfires, drought and disease – of course the science is not settled. In failing to see or refusing to admit the painfully simple distinction between the basic theory of the science of climate change that is consensual (which of course does not mean unanimous) and those parts that are necessarily uncertain and subject to vigorous debate, great mischief and public confusion have occurred either through calculated deception or an incapacity for clear thought.

Public confusion also rests on the failure to draw another altogether straightforward distinction. In an area of study as complex, technical and sophisticated as climate science, societies must rely on those with expertise, that is to say those with a proven depth of understanding. This will in general be found only among those who have graduated with a higher degree in one of the relevant disciplines and who have published their research in peer-reviewed journals. Over problems within the science of climate change, the opinions of those without true knowledge and understanding are worthless. As Clive Hamilton once put it so decisively, concerning those questions where authority rests on expertise, as it does with climate science, the issue for laypeople is not what to believe but who. Here, however, another obvious distinction needs to be made. If qualified scientists were deeply divided over the basic theory of climate change, citizens would not know what to believe and would have no way of deciding between contending views. Fortunately, on the basic theory, as we have seen, there is a consensus among the scientists. Accordingly, no rational layperson has any alternative but to accept the view that is consensual among them.

At this point we arrive at yet another, surprisingly common, confusion. I have argued that debate between unqualified people over the science of climate change is pointless, even absurd. However, this is not a claim, as it is so often mistakenly or mischievously misrepresented as being, that there ought not to be vigorous debate among citizens about the many vitally important non-scientific questions raised for all societies by what scientists tell us about climate change. For individual nations and for the international community there are very many questions that must be decided as a consequence of what the climate scientists report – how best to reduce emissions of greenhouse gases, at what pace they should be reduced, by what economic or political mechanism the reduction should be effected, how the costs of emissions reduction should be distributed within individual nations and across the international community, and so on. Such questions cannot be decided by climate scientists. They are, of course, proper subjects for open debate and democratic decision or international negotiation. To claim that there can be no serious debate about climate change science among laypeople is no different from saying that laypeople cannot usefully debate the science of nuclear physics. But just as we are obliged to debate the consequences that flow from the applications of nuclear physics, so are we obliged to debate how best to respond to what the scientists are warning with regard to climate change.

Here another basic distinction needs to be drawn. It is consensual among climate scientists that greenhouse gas emissions are warming the planet and that the warming will have many powerful, long-term damaging effects. There is, however, no agreement on the precise impact into the future of accelerating atmospheric greenhouse-gas levels. Some of the predictions of the best qualified climate scientists are relatively moderate although still dire – for example, a sea-level rise by 2100 of half a metre or less. Some of the best qualified, however, like James Hansen of NASA – who regards an ice-free earth and a sea level rise of seventy-five metres as a certainty if humankind continues to burn fossil fuels until their supply is exhausted – express profound alarm about what will happen unless radical action to curb carbon dioxide emissions is taken very soon. Just as unqualified laypeople cannot rationally debate the consensual conclusions of the climate scientists, so they cannot rationally know what to believe on those questions where the best qualified climate scientists disagree. To claim that because a scientist is alarmed about the future, he or she is an "alarmist" whose opinion can be therefore discounted is both arrogant and irresponsible.

In the discussion of climate change, the future of the earth and the human future are at stake. As we shall see, what the *Australian* has contributed on climate change under Chris Mitchell's watch is a truly frightful hotchpotch of ideological prejudice and intellectual muddle.

On 4 December 2010 the new environment editor at the *Australian*, Graham Lloyd, published a dramatic article of almost 4000 words entitled "*The Australian* answers its critics over its reporting of climate change."

Over the issue of global warming, the position of the newspaper had supposedly been maliciously distorted by its culture-war enemies. Chris Mitchell regretted not having sued Clive Hamilton in 2007 over offensive comments about him in the book *Scorcher*. He now intended to sue a journalism lecturer, Julie Posetti, over a tweet. "In essence," Mitchell explained to Lloyd, "we have allowed misleading polemics to frame the debate about our views and assumed smart people will see our real position simply by reading our paper." As it turned out, this had been a mistake. "There is no dispute," Lloyd wrote, "that *The Australian* has opened its news and opinion pages to a wide range of views on the existence and extent of climate change and what should be done about it. But the position taken by the newspaper in its daily editorial column, or leader, has been clear for well more [*sic*] than a decade." According to Mitchell, "this newspaper's editorial position on climate science and its longstanding support for a global response to limit greenhouse gas emissions" had been "misrepresented" for years. Lloyd sought to correct the historical record by cherry-picking passages from past *Australian* editorials.

The first editorial line Lloyd quoted was from 6 April 1995. It read: "The scientific consensus that global warming is occurring unnaturally, primarily as a result of industrial development and deforestation, is no longer seriously disputed in the world." The claim implicitly being made here is that under Mitchell the *Australian* continued to support the scientific consensus on climate change in its editorials. This is an outright falsehood. What follows is a selection from the scores of covertly and sometimes overtly denialist comments drawn from editorials over the Mitchell years.

On 12 January 2006 the *Australian* argued that "climate change may be a mirage." Two days later it explained that "for the prophets of gloom ... it is an article of the green faith that the world's climate is changing for the worse, because coal-fired power plants pump greenhouse gases into the atmosphere ... [W]hile environmental activists say science shows fossil fuels are responsible for a global warming crisis, which may be right, they could just as easily be wrong." On 15 March 2007, the *Australian* greeted the Martin Durkin documentary *The Great Global Warming Swindle* with enthusiasm. It welcomed what it called "the emergence of renewed scepticism within the scientific community" in "a debate that appears to have been hijacked by non-scientists, political advisers and bureaucrats." On 21 April 2008, the paper was heartened by the entry of at least two non-scientists into the debate over climate change science – the churchman Cardinal Pell and the political scientist Don Aitkin. Both were, it argued, "welcome voices of caution." The *Australian* claimed on 29 November 2008 that "if climate change is real – and 'if' is the operative word – every aspect of the phenomenon needs to be picked over and analysed with the utmost rigour." The entry into the debate on climate change science of the geologist Ian Plimer, who argued that he could demolish every single claim made by climate scientists, was even more warmly welcomed by the *Australian* than the entry of Pell or Aitkin. On 18 April 2009, the *Australian* argued that "as Professor Plimer demonstrates, expert irritation does not disguise the fact that the science is anything but settled." While the qualified scientists might genuinely believe that "there is a 90 per cent certainty that global warming is human-induced," as Plimer had explained "… they do not know. No one does." Ten days later the paper told its readers that "it remains to be proved that the rise" in "the levels of carbon dioxide" is "the major driver of global warming." The *Australian* seized upon the hacked climate scientist emails released on the eve of the Copenhagen conference. "In the past couple of weeks," it argued, "we have had a glimpse of the zealotry of the believers – and the gaps in their data – thanks to the exposure of the emails from the University of East Anglia." No editorials commented on the successive inquiries that subsequently cleared the scientists of wrongdoing. Despite a faux solemnity – "the evidence of sloppy science is depressing" – in truth the *Australian* appeared to be absolutely delighted when two embarrassing errors were discovered in the 1500-page Fourth Report of the IPCC. Indeed, it devoted no fewer than four editorials to the matter. On 19 January 2010, the *Australian* told its readers that the mistake over the Himalayan glaciers read like "a Monty Python skit"; on 22 January that for the IPCC "it does not get more humiliating" than this; and on 26 January that "public faith" in the IPCC "is evaporating" and that now "the premise behind global action – that the world is heating at a dangerous rate and that we can do something about it – needs to be rigorously tested." Finally, on 2 February 2010, it informed its readers that "the scientific evidence is being questioned around the world" and that "a fresh look at scientific data on climate change is needed before politicians can ask taxpayers to embark on schemes that could lead to trillions of dollars of lost wealth around the globe in coming decades."

Chris Mitchell inherited a newspaper that had accepted the consensual core of climate science. Although under his watch the *Australian* never formally abandoned this position, for nine years its editorials welcomed the anti–climate science challenges both of unqualified scientists and totally unqualified laypeople, consistently denied that the science was "settled," consistently failed to draw the distinction between the core theory of climate science that was consensual and the climate scientists' predictions about the future that were not, and expressed grave and growing doubts about the solidity even of those parts of climate science that were entirely consensual. By 2010, as we have seen, the longstanding if intermittent and inconsistent covert denialism of the *Australian* was perilously close to becoming overt. Mitchell's December 2010 claim that his paper had provided consistent editorial support for the findings of the climate scientists is simply false.

What, then, are we to make of Chris Mitchell's other claim, that his paper had offered "longstanding support for a global response to limit greenhouse gas emissions"?

Throughout the Mitchell years the *Australian* maintained, although not even here consistently, rather abstract support for eventual global action on climate change so long as the international price for carbon was modest and the plan was accepted by every major economy in the world. But when it came to practical schemes for global action that currently had international support and any chance of actually reducing emissions, the *Australian* was firmly opposed. By 2005 virtually all countries in the world had ratified the Kyoto Protocol. Of all the developed countries, only the United States and Australia had not. Kyoto was truly "the only game in town." The *Australian* was not merely an opponent of Kyoto. Its hostility was ferocious. On 29 July 2005, it described Kyoto as "power grabbing by the nations of old Europe – unrepentant polluters all – against the high-growth economies of the Asia-Pacific." On 13 December 2005, it described Kyoto as "madness" and as "rubbish." And on 4 August 2006, it called it "punitive." In essence the *Australian* opposed Kyoto because it did not require the booming developing economies like China, India and Brazil to cut their emissions. Its opposition was, however, extremely dishonest. The *Australian* almost invariably suggested to its readers that the non-involvement of the developing countries represented a permanent state of affairs. In truth the first phase of the Kyoto Protocol ended in 2012. After then it was hoped that, in a second stage, the developing countries would be drawn in.

As an alternative to Kyoto, the United States and Australia, under George W. Bush and John Howard, dreamed up a scheme called the Asia-Pacific Partnership on Clean Development and Climate. The Partnership did not set mandatory emissions reduction targets. It did not include "Old Europe." It did not aim to set an international price on carbon. Rather it proposed to reduce emissions principally through technology and technology transfer. At the inaugural meeting of the Partnership, in Sydney in January 2006, the *Australian* enthusiastically endorsed it. This support was not surprising: the *Australian* almost invariably supported George W. Bush's foreign policy. Moreover, one of the most consistent articles of faith of the *Australian* was that technology would solve humanity's dilemmas, which of course included the possible global warming problem.

As a putative scheme to reduce global emissions, the Asia-Pacific Partnership was almost self-evidently a fantasy. When the idea of the Partnership faded away with the election of Kevin Rudd and Barack Obama, the *Australian* returned to its support for a tepid international agreement, where the price on carbon was low, where all major economies were involved, where no mandatory targets were set, and where the sinister attempts by the impoverished countries of the world to use an international treaty to oversee a process of global wealth redistribution were properly resisted. When the Copenhagen conference more or less collapsed, the *Australian* was not at all dismayed. "Copenhagen was the last hurrah of zealots," it argued, "who have embraced climate change as a matter of faith, warning unbelievers they are dooming the planet, without offering any practical solutions." The lack of concern about what happened at Copenhagen is easy to explain. In several editorials the *Australian* had shown sympathy for Bjorn Lomborg's argument that any international action against climate change was a waste of money and destined to fail.

With its hostility to Kyoto, its support for the fantasy of the Asia-Pacific Partnership, its pleasure at the collapse of the Copenhagen conference and its attraction to the Lomborg idea that any global action would prove futile, the *Australian*'s record does not even remotely support Mitchell's claim that it had offered "longstanding support for a global response to limit greenhouse gas emissions."

What about Australia? Throughout the Mitchell years the paper argued consistently that Australia should primarily look after its own economic interests. We contributed only 1.4 per cent of global emissions. Nothing we could do would make any real difference. Acting alone or first or in advance of others was not wise. Even the idea of good global citizenship was suspect. The *Australian* was a tireless defender of the coal industry. "Mr Howard," it argued on 16 June 2004, "has seen the energy future and it consists of coal." This was a position from which the paper never wavered. The *Australian* regarded those who asked questions about the future of coal – like Bob Brown or Tim Flannery or James Hansen, who described coalmines as "factories of death" – as economically irrational and politically disordered. It regarded not only Australia's future, but also the world's, as tied inexorably and rightly to an accelerating consumption of coal for centuries to come. Although it was enthusiastic about Australia's natural gas, it regarded only nuclear power as an additional form of energy that would grow in significance in the future.

For these reasons the *Australian* argued that the greatest international contribution Australia could make to the problem of global warming was to export more of its uranium, including to India, despite the fact that it had not signed the non-proliferation treaty; to allow itself to become a global nuclear waste dump; but above all to become a world leader in the search for a "clean coal" solution to the problem of global warming. Usually the *Australian* used the term "clean coal" to describe geo-sequestration, a process for which it retained a confidence, though its enthusiasm appeared to diminish over time. Sometimes, however, extraordinarily enough, it described Australia's black anthracite coal as "clean." Australia, it argued, must never be reticent or ashamed about opening new coalmines or exporting more coal. For those who had plans for alternative energy sources, like solar, wind or tidal, the *Australian* had nothing but pity and contempt. Those sources would never support base-load electricity. It also opposed all mandatory renewable-energy targets as economically irrational.

Until the middle of 2007, the *Australian* was vehemently opposed to the Labor Party's determination to ratify Kyoto. Kyoto was job-destroying and a meaningless symbol. Rather suddenly, on 29 October 2007, it shifted ground. It now believed that "the nation and the government might as well have collected the brownie points" by ratifying Kyoto.

Before 2007, the *Australian* expressed doubts about any stand-alone national emissions trading scheme. On 2 November 2006, for example, it argued that a Labor proposal for an ETS would "lose jobs and investments to foreign markets." When the Howard government experienced an eleventh-hour pre-election ETS conversion, the *Australian*, however, offered its support, so long as the emissions reduction targets were extremely modest and businesses were generously compensated. In general it also supported the Rudd government's ETS proposals, especially as they became increasingly modest over time. At moments like the one when it thought that Rudd's ETS could no longer be distinguished from Howard's, or the one when Rudd's starting date was delayed from 2010 to 2011, the *Australian* cheered. The main criticism it made of Rudd was for his mistaken view that global warming was a "moral" issue and for the attacks he occasionally unleashed against the denialists in the Liberal Party, for example in his November 2009 Lowy Institute speech, where the *Australian* regarded "his hyperbolic rhetoric" as "polarising."

Throughout 2009 the *Australian* was enthusiastic about Kevin Rudd's refusal to negotiate with the Greens over the ETS and about Malcolm Turnbull's success in weakening it so that business interests were accommodated. It continually warned Rudd not to legislate in advance of the Copenhagen agreement. It was momentarily alarmed in November and early December 2009, when the denialists in the Liberal Party rebelled against Turnbull. On the ETS, it argued, Turnbull was "absolutely correct." The Liberals were facing their greatest crisis since 1949. If the Coalition moved to the Right, it would be "smashed" at the next election. The *Australian*'s principled support for a minimalist, market-based, business-friendly ETS did not, however, last long. In November 2009 the *Australian* had warned that if the Coalition opposed the ETS, it would be reduced to "dinosaur status." By May 2010 Abbott's destruction of the ETS was earning him the *Australian*'s praise. "By blocking the ETS, the opposition prevented Mr Rudd from taking Australia out on a limb, recklessly exposing the nation to economic risk."

On one question the editorialists at the *Australian* were completely consistent – their loathing and contempt for anyone who thought radical action on climate change was needed. Here the *Australian* did not show why the arguments of those calling for radical action were wrong. The fact that the level of atmospheric carbon dioxide was higher than it had been for 650,000 years and that it was increasing at an accelerating pace, or the concerns of climate scientists about the rate at which continental ice sheets, glaciers and the Siberian permafrost were melting, were, quite simply, never discussed in the *Australian*'s editorials. The only time Antarctic melt was mentioned – at the time of the collapse of the Wilkins ice shelf – the tone was breezily dismissive. The only time the melting of the Himalayan glaciers was mentioned was over the IPCC's error. Instead, all the *Australian* offered concerning the fears of the "deep greens," a.k.a. the climate scientists and environmentalists, was abuse taken from the standard songbook of the contemporary Right.

Here some detail is necessary. Those calling for radical action to curb greenhouse gas emissions were "greenhouse hysterics" (29 July 2005), "antediluvians" (9 August 2005), "prophets of doom" (14 January 2006), "neo-Arcadians" (31 March 2007), "deep-Green Luddites" (8 June 2007), "hair-shirted greenhouse penitents" (22 June 2007), "carpetbaggers" (17 December 2007), "utopian fantasists" (19 October 2009), "the hessian-bag brigade" (31 October 2009) and "zealots" (30 December 2009). According to the *Australian* the "deep greens" displayed "a head-in-the-sand mentality" (1 December 2006), a "revivalist fervour" (27 August 2008) and a "mindset" that was simultaneously "medieval" and "totalitarian" (14 June 2006, 12 March 2010). Such despicable people "would sell out the economy and their grandmothers" (27 May 2009). Tim Flannery was "a well-documented global warming extremist" (9 February 2007); Bob Brown would "not be satisfied until everyone is taking cold showers in the dark" (14 March 2007); while Al Gore was an "alarmist" afflicted by "hyperbolic visions of gloom" (15 February 2007, 29 March 2007). On 2 October 2008, the *Australian* asked: on "what planet" do these "deep greens" live? It did not occur to the *Australian* that the obvious answer to this question was that they lived on the imperilled earth.

How could the madness of these green totalitarians be explained? Not surprisingly, the *Australian* went straight to the clichés of the contemporary Anglophone Right. The deep greens had transferred discarded old religious impulses into environmental extremism. It pointed to "that radical and disproportionately loud fringe of greenies and leftists who treat environmentalism as a religion for whom humanity's sinful, decadent ways threaten to bring down the wrath of nature or the gods and must be changed." In addition, however, the paper, which remained frozen in its editor-in-chief's unreconstructed Cold War mentality, consistently regarded the "deep greens" as nothing but the communist Totalitarian Enemy reborn, whose secret hope was not to save the planet but to destroy capitalism and the Western way of life. The *Australian* argued that environmentalists who called for radical action to curb greenhouse gases formed what it called "the new frontline for anti-capitalist, anti-globalisation campaigners." Most importantly, however, it claimed that all such people were suffering from the disease of political correctness, the standard accusation of contemporary neoconservatives against the politics of the Left. In its editorial of 5 December 2009, the *Australian* defended the arch climate change denialist Ian Plimer. In one passage all three strands of its case against those calling for radical action can, rather neatly, be seen – their embrace of an absolutist politics as a substitute for abandoned religion, their disguised anti-capitalism, and their censorious political correctness.

> For too long, the debate on climate has mirrored the debates in this country in the 1990s, when any challenges to multiculturalism or the narrowly defined version of Aboriginal reconciliation were labelled right-wing or racist. Scientific sceptics, such as Ian Plimer, know how difficult it is to advance an argument against the quasi-religious fervour of climate change believers. That the passion and dogmatic belief that once defined organised religion have been replaced for some people by a commitment to reversing climate change is not surprising. As a response to what some see as excessive materialism in the West, fighting for the planet has become a way to scale back development, restrict free markets and redistribute wealth across the globe.

There was a significant problem here. Virtually every climate scientist is convinced that radical action to curb greenhouse gas emissions is vital.

In creating a new post–Cold War enemy camp – made up of climate scientists and environmentalists favouring such action – the *Australian* had broken with the values lying at the very centre of the Enlightenment, namely Science and the authority of Reason. At moments in its editorials the *Australian* half-recognised the implication of what it was saying. On one occasion it wrote disparagingly about "the scientist as savant" and on another about "the shortcomings of relying on experts." But in general the war on science was probably inadvertent. The *Australian's* wild, prolonged and abusive attack on the despised "other" it called the "deep greens" or the "true believers" was, then, not merely an assault on the ideal of civility in debate. It represented a great betrayal of the very values the newspaper imagined it embodied and upheld.

The *Australian's* total coverage of climate change under Chris Mitchell's watch cannot, of course, be captured by an analysis of the paper's editorial line. A more complex methodology is needed. What follows is an explanation of the one I employed. By the use of a Factiva newspaper database formula (contained in the notes to this essay) print-outs were obtained of all the climate change articles published by the *Australian* between January 2004 and April 2011. All the articles were read. Editorials were extracted for separate analysis. Letters to the editor were excluded, on the perhaps doubtful assumption that they represented a fair sample of the opinions of readers rather than editorial choice or prejudice. Climate change–related articles in the very many energy-industry supplements the *Australian* published – on oil, natural gas and coal – many of them edited by the former executive director of the Australian Petroleum Production and Exploration Association, Keith Orchison, were also excluded. Pieces contained in the "Cut and Paste" section and its predecessors were, however, included. Everyone who reads the *Australian* knows that daily mockery of opponents is one of the most potent means by which the paper's ideological and political agenda is advanced.

The remaining articles were divided into three categories. The first was formed from the news items and opinion columns written in support of the consensual core of the climate change science or the findings of the IPCC, or which supported the Kyoto Protocol and Australia's ratification of it, or which supported an Australian response at least as "radical" as the ETS mooted by the Howard government in 2007 and the Rudd government between 2008 and April 2010. I called this category "favourable to climate change action." A second was formed from the news items and opinion columns that opposed the consensual core of climate science, or the findings of the IPCC, or that opposed the Kyoto Protocol or Australia's adherence to it, or that were opposed to an Australian response at least as "radical" as the ETS prefigured or proposed by the Howard and Rudd governments between 2007 and early 2010. This category was called "unfavourable to climate change action." A third category was formed of climate change news items or opinion columns that were concerned with other matters or were simply neutral. After this third category was excluded, some 880 articles remained. Of these, about 180 were favourable to climate change action and 700 unfavourable. According to my calculations that means that under Chris Mitchell's editorship the *Australian*'s news items and opinion columns opposed action on climate change by a ratio of about four to one. Even if some of my judgments about the category in which some particular articles should fall were to be disputed – for example, I placed most but not all of political editor Dennis Shanahan's reports in the unfavourable category while Paul Kelly's contributions fell into both – I am convinced that no one who was objective could arrive at a ratio of less than three to one for news items and opinion columns unfavourable rather than favourable to my extremely, perhaps excessively, modest definition of what constitutes support for climate change action.

Of the opinion columns favourable to climate change action, the most frequently published authors were the regular left-winger Phillip Adams (8); the national affairs editor Mike Steketee (8, although later he contributed to "Inquirer"); and the former head of Greenpeace International Paul Gilding (6). Of the columns unfavourable to climate change action, the most published authors were the "all action is futile" sceptical economist

Bjorn Lomborg (25); the economics editor Alan Wood (22); the regular right-wingers Christopher Pearson (21), Janet Albrechtsen (14) and Frank Devine (8); the denialist geologist Bob Carter (9); the foreign editor Greg Sheridan (8); two employees of the neoliberal think-tank the Institute of Public Affairs, Alan Moran (8) and Tim Wilson (8); the former politician Gary Johns (7); and the neoliberal economists Alan Oxley (6) and Henry Ergas (5). Even more astonishing was the disproportionate number of columns or "Cut and Paste" extracts by denialist scientists, a group representing virtually no one published in peer-reviewed journals. Of the scientists rejecting the consensual view, the *Australian* published dozens of articles by Bob Carter, Michael Asten, William Kininmonth, Lord Monckton, Ian Plimer, Richard Lindzen, Jennifer Marohasy, Stewart Franks, Garth Paltridge, Dennis Jensen, David Evans, John Christy, David Bellamy and Nigel Calder. Of the scientists accepting the overwhelming consensus, it published Barry Brook (but principally in support of nuclear energy), James Hansen (but only to attack "cap and trade"), Andy Pitman (but only to disagree with Tim Flannery), Peter Doherty (but only in the *Australian Literary Review*), David Karoly and Kurt Lambeck. In the real world, scientists accepting the climate consensus view outnumber denialists by more than ninety-nine to one. In the *Alice in Wonderland* world of Chris Mitchell's *Australian* their contributions were outnumbered ten to one.

In a certain way, however, all this underestimates the kind of damage the *Australian* inflicted on the nation by its protracted war on climate science. During Chris Mitchell's editorship the *Australian* published scores of articles by people who claimed to know that the consensual view of the climate scientists was entirely bogus but who have not passed even a first-year university examination in one of the relevant disciplines. On the extraordinarily complex and technical questions of climate science, who cared about the ignorant opinions of Christopher Pearson or Janet Albrechtsen and the scores of other *Australian* contributors? Not only did such writers disagree with the consensual views of the climate scientists, they did so with a comical degree of self-confidence. Why was it important to know that Christopher Pearson believed that there was "something terribly galling about the federal government deciding to spend hundreds of millions of dollars on controlling emissions of what will turn out to be, in all probability, a perfectly harmless gas"; or that Janet Albrechtsen was of the opinion that there was "real possibility of global cooling should the sun revert to the lazier position associated with the Little Ice Age"; or that Senator Cory Bernardi had come to the view that "the more you read into this situation, the more the claims that man-made carbon dioxide emissions are responsible for our warming climate do not add up"; or that the Czech president Vaclav Klaus was convinced that "global warming is a myth and every serious person and scientist says so." No doubt such people would argue that if they are unqualified in the field of climate science, so am I. This is perfectly true. But to repeat Clive Hamilton's wise words, in an area such as this the question for laypeople is not what to believe, but who. I feel obliged to place my trust in the view of climate scientists. They place their trust in a handful of contrarians or cranks. To paraphrase Greg Sheridan, either every relevant scientific association in the United States is to be trusted on climate change, or Lord Monckton is. Take your pick. Democracy relies on an understanding of the difference between those questions that involve the judgment of citizens and those where citizens have no alternative but to place their trust in those with expertise. By refusing to acknowledge this distinction, in its coverage of climate change the *Australian* not only waged "war on science," the title the outstanding blogger at *Deltoid*, Tim Lambert, gives to his comprehensive series of postings, but also threatened the always vulnerable place of reason in public life.

In Tokyo, in November 2006, Rupert Murdoch announced his conversion to the cause of action on climate change. As he put it, "The planet deserves the benefit of the doubt." On no fewer than sixteen occasions in its editorials the *Australian* repeated its owner's phrase. Unlike over the invasion of Iraq, however, on this occasion the emperor's words did not bind the empire. In the United States, Fox News is the driving force of climate change denialism. Nor, despite its token agreement, did these words influence the behaviour of Murdoch's most important newspaper in Australia. Chris Mitchell's version of giving the planet the benefit of the doubt was to refuse to support the Kyoto Protocol; to argue against any significant Australian contribution to the global struggle to reduce emissions in advance of a universal agreement; to advocate increasing extraction, export and consumption of coal into the far-distant future; to support only the weakest possible version of an emissions trading scheme for Australia when that idea became bipartisan and then to abandon the idea when it was no longer so; to foster a public debate on the consensual core of climate science by providing a platform for a handful of contrarians, the consequence of which was to create general confusion and to undermine public confidence in science; to allow the news items and the opinion page of his newspaper to be overbalanced by a factor of four to one by writers unfavourable to action on climate change; and to maintain a permanent propaganda campaign of denigration against all those arguing for radical action to curb greenhouse gas emissions. On 7 November 2007, in New York, Rupert Murdoch told his employees that "climate change poses clear, catastrophic threats." If he had not been the chairman of News Corporation but a member of the Greens, for these words he would no doubt have been lampooned by the *Australian* as a deep-green alarmist or an anti-capitalist totalitarian.

KEVIN RUDD: "MORE GOUGH WHITLAM HEAVY THAN JOHN HOWARD LITE"

In the *Australian Financial Review* of March 2011 Mark Latham argued that the character of the *Australian* under Chris Mitchell was determined not by ideology but by ego. In my view it has been determined by both. In the case of the coverage of climate change the emphasis should be placed on the role of ideology in rationalising the defence of mining interests and helping to subvert reason. In the case of the *Australian*'s coverage of the rise and fall of Kevin Rudd the emphasis needs to be placed, rather differently, on the intersection of ideology and ego and the confusion in the mind of the editor-in-chief of the *Australian* of the personal and political dimensions of his relations with the Australian prime minister.

In my interview with Chris Mitchell, he was determined to debunk the idea that as a conservative or, as he puts it, a "right of centre" Murdoch newspaper, the *Australian* was willing to turn a blind eye to the mistakes and stumbles of the Howard government. In this he is no doubt correct. Before Mitchell's editorship, on the eve of the November 2001 election, it was the *Australian* that broke the "children overboard" story, namely that the Howard government's claim that Iraqi asylum seekers had thrown their own children into the ocean to blackmail their way to Australia was false. Under his editorship, on the eve of the October 2004 election, it was the *Australian* that broke the story of Mike Scrafton's phone conversations with John Howard that proved that the prime minister had misled the public when he claimed that no one from Defence had informed him before the 2001 election that the children-overboard story was a canard. Through the journalism of Caroline Overington, the *Australian* in 2006 pursued the Howard government vigorously over the story of the Australian Wheat Board's bribes to Saddam Hussein. And through the journalism of Hedley Thomas in 2007, it pursued it no less vigorously over its unprincipled behaviour in the case of Dr Mohammed Haneef, an Indian doctor groundlessly suspected of involvement in a British terrorist plot.

The claim that the *Australian* acted as an apologist for the Howard government is wrong.

It is not wrong, however, to claim that the newspaper was, on balance, a very strong and very significant supporter of the Howard government's economic and industrial relations policies and of its culture-war battles with the Left. This really does not need to be proven. In March 2006 the prime minister launched a book called *The Howard Factor*, put together by the *Weekend Australian*'s editor, Nick Cater. This is part of what he said:

> The *Australian* newspaper has been broadly supportive, generously so, of the government's economic reform agenda, a strong supporter consistently ... of industrial-relations reform. Its only criticism of the government is that it might not have gone far enough. The *Australian* was a strong but on occasions not uncritical supporter of taxation reform. It was a very strong supporter of our participation in the military operations in Iraq. On the other hand it's been a fierce, how shall I say, a fearless commentator on proceedings before the Cole Royal Commission [into the Australian Wheat Board] ... And it's been critical, although it's supportive generally, of our border-protection policies ...

According to John Howard, then, the *Australian* was a highly significant supporter of his government. The newspaper's relations with John Howard were straightforward and are now uncontroversial. To put it mildly, the same cannot be said about the *Australian*'s strongly supportive, then turbulent and, in the end, lethal relations with Kevin Rudd and his government. Without some brief biographical detail at this point the strange story of what happened and why will remain unnecessarily opaque.

By 1994 Chris Mitchell and his first wife, Deborah Cassrels, had separated. In 1996 Mitchell was re-married to another journalist, Christine Jackman. Rudd had previously been friendly with Jackman and also, although less closely, with Mitchell. Now, from time to time, Rudd and his wife, Thérèse Rein, saw Mitchell and Jackman socially. Mitchell was editor-in-chief of the *Courier Mail*. Rudd was a former member of the Department of Foreign Affairs, a former senior state public servant as head of the Department of the Premier and Cabinet in the Goss Labor government, and a recently unsuccessful candidate for the ALP in the Brisbane seat of Griffith. When Rudd was a public servant, Mitchell's paper had occasionally criticised him. After he left the public service, Rudd, and also his daughter, Jessica, wrote columns for Mitchell's paper. In 1998 Rudd won the seat of Griffith. In mid-2002 Mitchell moved to Sydney to take up the editorship of the *Australian*. Relations between the families continued. In 2006 Chris Mitchell and Christine Jackman, who had moved with her husband from the *Courier Mail* to the *Australian*, asked Rudd and his wife to be godparents of their first child, Riley. Rudd agreed. By now Rudd had his sights on the leadership of the Labor Party, which was languishing under Kim Beazley. And by now Mitchell had decided to support Rudd in his leadership bid.

So far as I am aware, Rudd has never spoken publicly about the character of his relations with Mitchell. Mitchell, however, recently explained to the journalist Sally Neighbour, who was writing a profile of him for the *Monthly*, "I'm aware throughout my relationship with him there have been times when I've used him and there've been times when he's used me …" This is a curious remark. The use that an ambitious politician can make of a friendly newspaper editor is self-evident. But what use-value did Rudd have for Mitchell? Did Mitchell think that by supporting Rudd he could become a player in Australian politics, helping move the Labor Party rightwards? Did he simply enjoy the prospect of being a political king-maker, as Sally Neighbour suggests? In the course of research for this essay I heard two comments about the relationship between Mitchell and Rudd that seemed to me illuminating. One was that they were "obsessed" with each other. The other was that Mitchell was driven throughout by a desire for control.

Mitchell's decision to support Rudd's bid to become Labor leader raised some obvious problems. It is true that Rudd belonged to the Right faction of the ALP and that earlier, as the head of the premier's department in Queensland, he had earned himself a reputation as a ruthless bureaucratic rationalist. But it is also true that his worldview was far distant from that of Chris Mitchell. In his bid for the leadership Rudd published two essays in the *Monthly*. In these he revealed that he was a disciple of the Lutheran anti-Nazi martyr Dietrich Bonhoeffer and a Christian social democrat. As such, he was the only Labor Party frontbencher who was willing to engage John Howard in combat over the most sensitive issues in the culture wars: asylum seekers, Aboriginal reconciliation and the moral dimension of climate change. Even before the *Monthly* articles, in his maiden parliamentary speech in 1998 and elsewhere, Rudd revealed that he had entered politics as an enemy of the father of contemporary neoliberalism, Friedrich Hayek, and of neoliberalism's hostility to the idea at the heart of contemporary social democracy, the creation of a substantial, generous and elaborate welfare state. Such ideas were anathema to Mitchell. In Mitchell's support of the Rudd leadership bid, their ideological differences must have been blurred or concealed. More than this, however, needs to be said. Unlike most Australian participants in politics and the media, both Mitchell and Rudd live in a world of ideas. If their relations were to prosper in the long term, one or other would have to change. Given both the ideological requirements placed on all his editors by Rupert Murdoch and the unfeigned enthusiasm for the neoconservative and neoliberal Murdoch house philosophy displayed by Mitchell, change could only come from Kevin Rudd. There was, however, no reason to believe that it would. Rudd's worldview, as a Christian social democrat, went deep.

Rudd won the Labor leadership from Beazley in late 2006. Throughout 2007 Mitchell offered support. It began seriously on 10 February with a very favourable profile written for the *Weekend Australian Magazine* by Christine Jackman. Jackman told us that Rudd was looking forward to playing with Howard's mind in the build-up to the election. At the beginning of the article she raised the standard objections to Rudd's bid to be prime minister, only to dismiss them:

The MP who is too inexperienced to be prime minister is, simultaneously, the man who, as head of Queensland premier Wayne Goss's Cabinet Office in the early '90s, helped run a state at one of the most challenging times in its history; his cutting and restructuring of Queensland's public service earned him the moniker Dr Death. Dr Death, the political enforcer, is simultaneously the urbane intellectual who can pen a 5000-word treatise on the place of religious faith in politics. And that owlish intellectual is also the consummate media performer who can field questions from the Canberra press gallery about the UN Security Council Resolution 661 in the AWB scandal, then turn up to perform in a hokey rap video of "Where is the Love?" for Breakfast TV.

Although the *Australian* mentioned that Christine Jackman's "family have known the Rudd family since before Rudd entered politics," it did not tell its readers that Jackman was Mitchell's wife or that Rudd had become the godfather of their son in the previous year. Already, in the *Australian*'s coverage of the ascent of Kevin Rudd, the line between the personal and the political had been blurred.

In April, Rudd visited Rupert Murdoch in New York, an obligatory pilgrimage for any Labor leader. I have been told by several insiders that the pair never really hit it off. According to one account, both were more accustomed to delivering speeches than to making conversation. According to another, Rudd privately detested Murdoch's right-wing ideology and was temperamentally unwilling to crawl. What is, however, undeniable is that both before he took office and indeed throughout the period of the Rudd government, personal and political relations between Rupert Murdoch and Kevin Rudd were decidedly cool. Nonetheless, as Mitchell later pointed out, this did not in any way prevent his newspaper from giving both Kevin Rudd and Wayne Swan, throughout 2007, generous space to argue their case.

This support was not unqualified. By far the most serious criticism the

Australian advanced against the Rudd Opposition was its decision to abandon WorkChoices, which, in characteristic timbre, Paul Kelly argued had destroyed its credibility as an alternative economic manager. Mitchell, too, was clearly very troubled by Labor's abandonment of WorkChoices and also by the supposed influence of the Victorian Left – Julia Gillard in industrial relations, Senator Kim Carr in industry policy – on whom Rudd had relied to win the Labor leadership. He was, however, heartened by Rudd's amendment to Labor's Fair Work alternative, and even more by Rudd's description of himself, in a pre-election television advertisement, as "an economic conservative … when it comes to public finances," which the *Australian* not unreasonably misunderstood. Rudd thought of himself as a fiscal conservative, someone concerned about the budget bottom line across the business cycle. An economic conservative, in Mitchell's understanding, is a neoliberal with a fundamental faith in the beneficence of the market and an equally fundamental suspicion about the economic role of government.

At this time I gained a personal insight into the Mitchell view of Rudd. In the *Monthly* I had written a series of commentaries putting the case for a change of government on standard anti-Howard culture-war grounds. Against the scepticism about Rudd that was growing on the Left, I argued that his "me-tooism" was to some extent a front. Mitchell sent me an email. He assured me that Rudd was a genuine conservative. He knew him personally. I did not. And in public, on 27 October, he published a revealing editorial, entitled "Daydreaming Left is in for a big surprise." The Left believed Rudd would alter the course of the nation set by Howard. They were wrong. Rudd had "spent the last eleven months signing himself up to Howard's policy agenda." Rudd was "fundamentally conservative." His "secret" had been "to outflank the Prime Minister on the Right rather than attack him from the Left." The policy distance between Labor and the Coalition had never been narrower than it was at present. "Of course," the editorial concluded sarcastically, "we may be wrong about Mr Rudd. He may turn out to be the most convincing actor ever to walk the Australian political stage and once in office might reveal his true identity as a starry-eyed activist waiting to unleash a Whitlamesque program of social reform." But then again he may not. The *Australian* was willing to make only one firm prediction. "The agenda of a Rudd government is likely to be much closer to the position advocated in the editorial columns of this newspaper than the outdated, soft-left manifesto supported by our broadsheet rivals." Decoded, what Mitchell was saying here was simple. Rudd is my man.

In the coming election Rupert Murdoch leant towards Howard. In interviews with both Sally Neighbour and me, Mitchell made a point of informing us that he had to convince Murdoch to allow the *Australian* to support Labor. He succeeded. By election day, 23 November, at the end of a series of characteristically self-important but uncharacteristically equivocal and conflicted editorials – "Determined Rudd is on message," "One more time or once too many?" "Time to think about the future" – and with a major caveat over industrial relations, the *Australian* finally commended Kevin Rudd to its readers.

During its first months, relations between the Rudd government and the *Australian* were generally cordial. The *Australian* was not greatly fussed when Rudd went to Bali to ratify Kyoto. It gave strong support to the government's long-overdue apology to the stolen generations. It even contained its natural rancour during the prime minister's 2020 Summit, where Kevin Rudd was hailed as hero by the nation's one thousand "best and brightest." Insofar as there was any bad blood in the early months between the *Australian* and the prime minister, it developed over an article written by John Lyons on 21 June 2008 – "Captain Chaos and workings of the inner circle" – which identified the weaknesses in Rudd's prime ministerial office, the shortcomings of Kevin Rudd as a manager of cabinet business, and the resentments that were building because of the unreasonable demands that the prime minister was making on the Commonwealth public service. On both sides this article is still remembered. At the *Australian* Chris Mitchell thinks of it as prophetic and prescient. Rudd's supporters think of it as profoundly unbalanced and a portent of the vindictiveness to come. They believed at the time, and indeed still believe, that Mitchell deeply resented the fact that they were unwilling, as a matter of principle, to give reporters at the *Australian* the kind of privileged position they had supposedly become accustomed to under Howard (a position which, incidentally, in my interview with Dennis Shanahan and Matthew Franklin, both hotly denied).

The next trouble between the Rudd government and the *Australian* erupted in October 2008. Once more, as so often in Mitchell's relations with Rudd, the line between the personal and the political was blurred. On 10 October, after a business dinner in Sydney, Rudd invited Mitchell to Kirribilli House. At about 10 p.m. George W. Bush called. Rudd spoke to him on a speakerphone with a member of his private office taking notes. By the time the call had concluded, Mitchell was the only guest remaining. Fifteen days later the *Australian* carried an exclusive front-page story detailing the conversation. Ostensibly, the story flattered Rudd. It claimed he had been crucial in convincing Bush to summon a meeting of the G20 rather than the G7 in the emergency response to the global financial crisis. Halfway through the story, however, readers learnt that to the amazement of Rudd, Bush had inquired: "What's the G20?" The embarrassing story circulated swiftly around the world; it seemed to confirm the popular stereotype that Bush was an idiot and an ignoramus. Not surprisingly, the president was seriously displeased. His staff informed the *Washington Post* that it was quite false, as seems to have been the case. As Lenore Taylor and David Uren discovered, Bush had been working on G20 matters two days earlier. Perhaps Bush simply had trouble with Rudd's Australian accent. Whatever the explanation, when Rudd arrived at the G20 summit in Washington, he was greeted extremely frostily by the US president.

Rudd had by now been placed in an impossible political situation. On the one hand, he denied that Bush had made the embarrassing remark to him. On the other, he pointedly refused to deny that he or his staff had leaked the story to the *Australian*, which no less pointedly continued to affirm the accuracy of its report. There is little doubt that the G20 story did Rudd some real harm. As Michelle Grattan of the *Age* remarked, "Questioning on the leak has become the first substantial challenge to Rudd on integrity grounds." Among right-wing journalists the common view was that Rudd had indeed conveyed the details of the conversation and Bush's supposed gaffe to Mitchell. They claimed that Rudd was a notorious "big-noter." No one knew whether the story that appeared in the *Australian* represented a breach of confidence by Mitchell and why the story was not reported for fifteen days. Among those who are in a position to know, opinion is still divided on whether the incident did permanent damage to Rudd's relations with Mitchell. I am almost certain it did not.

Political insiders to whom I have spoken, and two senior political journalists at the *Australian*, Dennis Shanahan and Matthew Franklin, agreed, however, on one matter. Towards the end of 2008 or in early 2009 relations between the prime minister and the editor-in-chief of the *Australian* did deteriorate noticeably. One possible explanation is a breakdown of the personal relationship between Rudd and Mitchell. Rumours circulated, reported later in the *Canberra Times*, that Kevin Rudd and Thérèse Rein provided counsel to Christine Jackman during the bitter breakdown of her marriage to Chris Mitchell and that Mitchell resented this. A second possible explanation, which I think is far more important, concerns Rudd's authorship of a long essay on the global financial crisis that he wrote during his summer holiday in January 2009 and that was published in the February edition of the *Monthly*.

Kevin Rudd's essay was, strangely enough, the first substantial analysis published in Australia of the reasons for the crisis of the global financial system following the collapse of Lehman Brothers in September 2008. Rudd had a longstanding intellectual interest in the financial products known as derivatives, whose fatal entanglement with the US housing market was at the core of the collapse. His essay traced the ways in which the radical deregulation of the US financial markets, inspired by the neo-liberal ascendancy in Washington, had triggered a process which rapidly brought the world economy to its knees. As a moralist, he linked the global financial catastrophe to the conspicuous greed of the Wall Street brokers and bankers who had paid themselves billions of dollars in bonuses as reward for their involvement in the derivatives trade. As an historian, Rudd argued that just as stagflation had killed off the thirty-year Keynesian era following World War II, so now would the global financial crisis discredit the thirty-year neoliberal era presided over by Friedrich Hayek. In the crisis everyone, including the exquisitely hypocritical neo-liberal economists and Wall Street brokers and bankers, who believed in the magic of the market, had looked for swift action from governments. Rudd thought that in the new era global financial markets would have to be far better regulated, and that in individual countries a more healthy balance would have to be struck between governments and markets. It was the historic task of social democracy to prevent capitalism from "cannibalising" itself. If it failed to do so, the door might be opened for the re-emergence of the extremes of Left and Right, as it had been during the last true crisis of the global economy, the Great Depression.

There are two reasons why this essay offended Mitchell. As a fiercely competitive newspaperman and as someone who felt that Rudd was in his debt, Mitchell was almost certainly seriously displeased that the essay had been sent to the *Monthly* and not to the *Australian*. When the answer to it, written by Malcolm Turnbull, was published by the *Australian*, its gossip columnist gloated. Far more importantly, however, in Mitchell's eyes the essay was heresy. He had constructed in his mind an image of Kevin Rudd – the man he believed he had helped become prime minister and commended to his paper's owner – as a right-wing neoliberal. Here was the definitive or canonical proof that he was wrong.

The *Australian* greeted the publication of Rudd's *Monthly* essay with instant artillery fire. "Cut and Paste" on 2 February was devoted to it. Rudd's epitaph for neoliberalism – "The time has come ... to proclaim that the great neo-liberal experiment of the past 30 years has failed" – was placed against similar-sounding comments by Noam Chomsky and Hugo Chavez. What more needed to be said? It turned out quite a good deal.

Over the next year the *Australian* published scores of articles and editorials revealing hostility to the Rudd essay, as well as a tiny handful that were friendly.

Among the *Australian*'s leading commentators, only Paul Kelly was thoughtful and respectful. For almost everyone else the Rudd essay provoked little but derision and abuse. Only some highlights can be recorded here. Early on, Rudd was accused of plagiarism by Matthew Franklin. When a subsequent article of Rudd's was rejected by the premier international-relations journal in the United States, *Foreign Affairs*, the *Australian* experienced the pleasures of schadenfreude. Commentary from politicians in the *Australian* was almost uniformly abusive. Tony Abbott described the essay as "pretentious and self-serving twaddle." Malcolm Turnbull described it as "absurd" and as a "slightly more genteel version of a foaming-in-the-mouth radical like Hugo Chavez." For his part, the embittered former NSW treasurer Michael Costa thought it was aimed squarely at "the cultural Left that dominates what passes for an intelligentsia in Australia." By comparison, the dismissive comments of John Howard were almost civil.

It was not only the commentary by politicians that was almost uniformly hostile and indeed nasty. Henry Ergas was characteristically condescending: "What do we owe a prime minister? At the very least, to take what he says seriously. Mr Rudd, in his recently published essay on 'The Global Financial Crisis' ... does not make that easy." David Burchell was, no less characteristically, pompous. He thought that thanks to Rudd's essay, "we're sojourning in our own parallel economic universe, made out of equally fabulous materials to Columbus's." Most bilious, however, was the historian Greg Melleuish, who (rather ungrammatically) likened Rudd to Joseph Stalin on the basis that "the only examples of leaders in power devoting themselves to issuing manifestos on such matters would appear to be totalitarian regimes." Several commentators accused Rudd of rank hypocrisy. Thérèse Rein by now ran a highly successful international employment agency. Had the prime minister not profited personally from the neoliberal policies he spurned? Jane Andrew, for example, argued that, "It is hard not to notice that the Rudd–Rein household has benefited handsomely from the neo-liberal loot."

More commonly, Rudd was accused of dissimulation. In one of her four columns devoted to Rudd's essay, Janet Albrechtsen, who with her normal restraint had previously described Rudd's article as "wicked," "arrogant," "hubris-filled," "cheap," "cunning," "deliberately dishonest" and "hypo-critical," claimed that Rudd had written his essay solely as a political ploy to cosy up to the Labor Left. "[H]is attack on free markets is not about ideas at all. It's crude politics, end of story." Albrechtsen's evidence was that when Rudd had appeared at the market fundamentalist think-tank the Centre for Independent Studies, he had never uttered a word in criticism of neoliberalism. "Believe me, we would have noticed." Albrechtsen was apparently unaware that Rudd had told the parliament in his maiden speech that one of his reasons for entering politics was distaste for the ideas of Friedrich Hayek. Like Albrechtsen, Greg Sheridan thought Rudd was only pretending not to be a neoliberal. His reason for writing such nonsense was purely political. While his account of the failure of US financial deregulation was unexceptional, the prime minister knew full well that the essay's broader "historical and intellectual claims" were "entirely fraudulent." Four weeks later Sheridan interviewed the South Korean president, Lee Myung-bak. He told Sheridan that he agreed with the thrust of Rudd's essay. Apparently the president had not noticed its domestic political purpose or its entire intellectual fraudulence.

In its editorials, the *Australian* shared the Albrechtsen–Sheridan interpre-tation. As the paper argued on 12 March 2009: "Nobody, except perhaps Robert Manne in *The Monthly*, really thinks Mr Rudd, in his essay deriding the market economics of neo-liberalism, 'could actually believe deeply what he wrote.'" There was, however, a problem for the *Australian* with the Rudd-is-only-pretending-not-to-be-a-neoliberal hypothesis. If Rudd did not believe what he wrote in his essay on the global financial crisis, and if his purposes were purely political, why did the newspaper publish perhaps a hundred articles and editorials over the next eighteen months debunking Rudd's thesis and attacking him for arguing it?

On 27 October 2007, the *Australian* in its editorial "Daydreaming Left is in for a big surprise," had argued that Rudd was a true conservative. By conservative what it meant, in large part, was that he was a true market liberal or, in Rudd's parlance, neoliberal. In writing his essay on the global financial crisis, Rudd had shown that the *Australian*'s earlier interpretation of him was based on a fundamental misunderstanding. Rudd might not, after all, be Mitchell's man. At a personal level, rather than admit that he had misjudged Rudd, Mitchell might have convinced himself that he had been deceived. If so, it was easy to find a political rationalisation for this anger. Rudd's political and ideological trajectory represented a clear and present danger for Australia.

The new concern about Rudd was spelt out clearly in an editorial published on 12 March 2009, "First leader to the centre wins." Rudd had been elected as a "fresh face presenting himself as an economic conservative." To get to the top he had relied on the Victorian Labor Left. He was still beholden to them. The *Australian* was particularly concerned about the performance of Kim Carr in his industry portfolio and Julia Gillard in industrial relations, who had "delivered big-time for her ACTU and Labor Left colleagues an industrial relations system that takes the nation back pre-Howard, pre-Keating and pre-Hawke to the rigid, centralised system of the 1970s." Halfway through his term Rudd's re-election prospects were being imperilled by what the *Australian* described with extraordinary hyperbole as "industrial relations and industry policy seemingly run out of a leftist ideological handbook from the Whitlam era." Rudd's "lurch to the Left" was extraordinary. If Rudd wanted to save himself, he needed now to turn Right.

As there was no sign that Rudd had taken this advice, on 9 September the *Australian* returned to this theme, in an editorial it called "Popular PM, or a true reformer?" Rudd was "arguably the most electorally secure politician in a quarter of a century." This popularity presented him with a choice. Either he could be a reformer or a failure. For the newspaper, reformer was code for neoliberal. By now the *Australian* was very worried about the identity of the prime minister. What had happened to the gritty Queensland public servant? In his recent essays, it was argued, Rudd had "reinvented himself as a Dietrich Bonhoeffer-inspired social democrat, arguing that this is the moment for a return to such governments." He needed "a reality check about the return to the failed social democratic model he has touted in recent essays." The idea that Rudd had reinvented himself as a Bonhoeffer social democrat was seriously strange. Rudd had spoken against Hayek in his maiden speech in 1998. He had written on Bonhoeffer in the *Monthly* in 2006. Mitchell had wilfully misunderstood him. It was not the daydreaming Left but the editor-in-chief of the *Australian* who had experienced a big surprise. Rudd was officially a disappointment, or indeed something worse.

From mid-2009 relations between Rudd and the *Australian* were very bad. Rudd's supporters had even now begun to count the number of times they were attacked. In June 2009 Rudd claimed that the *Australian* had published more than sixty articles coming to more than 60,000 words attacking his *Monthly* essay. In a public meeting in October he laughed when he was tackled on the cost of his climate change legislation and discovered that an article in the *Australian* was the questioner's source. The *Australian* was not objective. It had opposed government action on climate change for years. "The editor has said that he edits a right-wing newspaper and so he does." As was his wont, Mitchell soon retaliated. In an article by Geoff Elliott and Peter van Onselen, Rudd was described as an "acid-mouthed tyrant" who "is known to yell and curse at editors for stories that run contrary to his tightly controlled agenda." Chris Uhlmann's description of Rudd as a politician with "the bearing of a parson and the soul of a dictator" was quoted approvingly. So was Rupert Murdoch's rather ominous remark that Rudd was "too sensitive for his own good." Mitchell was interviewed for the story, something that by then happened frequently. He pointed out that he described his paper not as right-wing but centre-right. Rudd's distortion was typical of his habit of "verballing." Mitchell interpreted Rudd's October rebuke as a sign that he resented the scrutiny that only his newspaper, and certainly not its Fairfax rivals, supplied.

The battle was on. Although it was formally "off the record," Rudd appears to have spoken frankly to Peter Hartcher of the *Sydney Morning Herald* in November 2009 about the breakdown of his relations with Chris Mitchell. Hartcher learned that Rudd had had a reasonably friendly three-hour meeting with Rupert Murdoch in September in New York. He learned that Rudd's relations with other News Limited papers remained cordial. It was only relations with the *Australian* that had soured. Hartcher referred to what was called the paper's "front-page bellicosity." This was not imagined. At the end of 2009 the Rudd camp took a tally. In 2008 there had been 115 front-page stories critical of the Rudd government. In 2009 there had been 176. The main topics were climate change, industrial relations, economic management, asylum seekers and, from June, the $16.2 billion stimulus for the Building the Education Revolution program, which one front-page story had actually labelled "evil." For the accelerating hostility, Hartcher reported, Rudd held Mitchell's personal animosity entirely to blame.

In January 2010 the *Australian* made Kevin Rudd its Australian of the Year. The paper acknowledged that under the prime minister's leadership and the bold stimulus package he had introduced at time of emergency, Australia had survived the global financial crisis better than the other Anglophone democracies. "Far from being mugged by the global financial crisis, Mr Rudd rose to the occasion and displayed the leadership qualities that have defined Australians of the Year since the award was launched 40 years ago." Given the hostility of the *Australian* to Kevin Rudd and his government in recent months, the honour was greeted by Rudd's supporters with general merriment. Sally Neighbour reports that his personal staff interpreted it as an act of pure political Machiavellianism, giving the *Australian* "the licence to kick the shit out of you for the rest of the year." If that was what members of Rudd's staff anticipated, they were certainly not wrong.

Between January and late April 2010, the *Australian*'s front-page belli-cosity continued with a vengeance. There were many stories trying to document the dangers of the Rudd government's industrial relations policy. Almost all concerned matters that were either ephemeral or trivial or both. Clearly the *Australian* was having trouble admitting that the aban-donment of WorkChoices had been both an economic and a political success. Many front-page stories detailed the deepening troubles facing the Rudd government with the accelerating arrival on Christmas Island of asylum-seeker boats. This was hardly surprising. Rudd had abandoned John Howard's cruel but effective "Pacific Solution," with predictable consequences. Moreover, unlike Malcolm Turnbull, Tony Abbott with his catchcry of "stop the boats" was exploiting without restraint the political potential of the boat arrivals. The image the coverage created was of a government in crisis and unravelling. In giving great prominence to this issue, very damaging to the Rudd government, the *Australian*, however, could not really be criticised. The issue was neither ephemeral nor trivial. Nor could it be criticised for the prominence it gave on its front page to stories dealing with the Rudd government's $2.45 billion home-insulation stimulus program, administered by Peter Garrett and Mark Arbib. In a lightly regulated industry, hundreds of cowboys took advantage of the money on offer. There were four deaths by electrocution and more than ninety house fires. As the prime minister admitted in late February, this was an administrative failure for which he and his government had to accept full responsibility and blame.

Far more problematic, however, was the *Australian*'s parallel campaign against the $16.2 billion Building the Education Revolution stimulus program. There were undoubtedly some major cost blow-outs, especially in the NSW education department's administration of the scheme. There were also several embarrassing construction choices, like projects for schools soon to be closed down, which it was of course right to report. However, to depict the BER program as a straightforward catastrophe like the insulation program was untrue.

Never again miss an issue. Subscribe and save.

☐ **1 year subscription** (4 issues) only $49 (incl. GST). Subscriptions outside Australia $79.
All prices include postage and handling.

☐ **2 year subscription** (8 issues) only $95 (incl. GST). Subscriptions outside Australia $155.
All prices include postage and handling.

☐ Tick here to commence subscription with the current issue.

PAYMENT DETAILS Enclose a cheque/money order made out to Schwartz Media Pty Ltd.
Or please debit my credit card (MasterCard, Visa or Amex accepted).

CARD NO. ☐☐☐☐ ☐☐☐☐ ☐☐☐☐ ☐☐☐☐

EXPIRY DATE   /   AMOUNT $

CARDHOLDER'S NAME

SIGNATURE

NAME

ADDRESS

EMAIL   PHONE

tel: (03) 9486 0288 **fax:** (03) 9486 0244 **email:** subscribe@blackincbooks.com **www.quarterlyessay.com**

An inspired gift. Subscribe a friend.

☐ **1 year subscription** (4 issues) only $49 (incl. GST). Subscriptions outside Australia $79.
All prices include postage and handling.

☐ **2 year subscription** (8 issues) only $95 (incl. GST). Subscriptions outside Australia $155.
All prices include postage and handling.

☐ Tick here to commence subscription with the current issue.

PAYMENT DETAILS Enclose a cheque/money order made out to Schwartz Media Pty Ltd.
Or please debit my credit card (MasterCard, Visa or Amex accepted).

CARD NO. ☐☐☐☐ ☐☐☐☐ ☐☐☐☐ ☐☐☐☐

EXPIRY DATE   /   AMOUNT $

CARDHOLDER'S NAME   SIGNATURE

ADDRESS

EMAIL   PHONE

RECIPIENT'S NAME

RECIPIENT'S ADDRESS

tel: (03) 9486 0288 **fax:** (03) 9486 0244 **email:** subscribe@blackincbooks.com **www.quarterlyessay.com**

Delivery Address:
37 LANGRIDGE St
COLLINGWOOD VIC 3066

Quarterly Essay
Reply Paid 79448
COLLINGWOOD VIC 3066

Delivery Address:
37 LANGRIDGE St
COLLINGWOOD VIC 3066

Quarterly Essay
Reply Paid 79448
COLLINGWOOD VIC 3066

In a program as large as this, whose purpose was to provide an emergency stimulus to the building industry, mistakes were inevitable. In July 2011 the investment banker Brad Orgill delivered a comprehensive report on the program to the Gillard government. On balance he regarded it as a success. Clearly there were important problems in the way the education departments in New South Wales and Victoria had administered their part of the program. Yet in a program of 23,670 separate building projects, there had been only 332 complaints. The program, in Orgill's view, had succeeded in providing economic stimulus. Moreover, Orgill discovered widespread gratitude for the new school buildings across the country. And not only that. The *Australian*'s campaign had characterised "Building the Education Revolution" as a classic case of Big Government failure. Orgill argued that in the cases of the NSW and Victorian governments' poor performance, the main cause of the difficulties was precisely the opposite. Problems had occurred because, in the era of neoliberalism and small government, the public-works capacity in New South Wales and Victoria had been "hollowed out." When the final Orgill report appeared, on its front page and in its editorial the *Australian* seriously misrepresented its balance and almost entirely ignored its positive conclusions. Readers of the paper would have imagined that Orgill had found the BER program to have been a resounding failure.

In January 2010 Kevin Rudd had been the "obvious choice" as Australian of the Year for the way his government's bold stimulus spending had saved the nation from recession. Between early February and late April 2010, on ideological grounds, the *Australian* arrived at the opposite conclusion about the two largest stimulus programs. On 11 February it pointed out that the home-insulation "bungle" provided proof, if any were needed, "that governments do better when they allow market forces and commercial realities to determine consumer demand." On 20 February it launched an attack on the idea of "Big Canberra." Rudd was "intent on inserting government at the centre of the Australian economy." He needed to re-learn "the limits of government." Stimulus spending, which the paper soon argued was double what it should have been, had provided "an excuse to return to the big-spending habits of the past." Yet it was even worse than mere big spending. Readers were soon to learn that the home-insulation and schools building programs were reminiscent of "the corruption and distortions that defined centrally managed economies such as the Soviet Union."

The problem here was the prime minister. Readers learned that he had undergone "a dramatic transformation from neo-Right Queensland bureaucrat to social-democratic Prime Minister." Voters had liked him when he was "John Howard-lite in 2007." They might once have "indulged Mr Rudd's penchant for writing essays on social-democracy." Their tolerance had worn out. Rudd must "get back in touch with who he really is" – "a right-wing Labor Prime Minister" – or he would pay a very heavy price. For a moment, in the health debate with Tony Abbott that Rudd won comprehensively, the *Australian* thought it got a glimpse of the true Queensland right-wing, bureaucratic Kevin Rudd of its imaginings. On 24 March the editorial was called "Welcome back, Mr Rudd." The welcome did not last long.

In late April Kevin Rudd took two steps that in combination would bring him down: the postponement of the emissions trading scheme and the announcement of his government's intention to introduce a mining industry super profits tax. The response of the *Australian* was instructive in both cases.

The *Australian* had urged the Rudd government on a number of occasions to abandon the ETS. On 2 March in an editorial called "Time to turn the ETS off?" it argued: "It looks like time for Kevin Rudd to consider turning off the emission trading scheme's political life support and accept that it was too pure an idea for the dirty world of international politics." And yet, when the Rudd government decided to defer the scheme for two years, the response of the *Australian* was not pleasure or praise, but hostility and scorn. In an editorial published on 28 April called "So that's what he meant by a great moral challenge," it argued that the prime minister's "humiliation" was "complete." He had "capitulated" to Tony Abbott. He had no "clear alternative" policy. This was "no way to handle a policy reversal that leaves business high and dry and voters bewildered. In 2007, Mr Rudd campaigned on climate change. This time round, he will try to bury it. After high expectations on the issue, the Prime Minister will only have himself to blame if voters see it differently." I have been following politics for four decades. This is the first instance I can recall of a government being pilloried by a newspaper for following its advice.

Yet the significance of this coverage was nothing in comparison to the reaction to the announcement of a super profits tax on mining proceeds. For reasons that will soon become clear, it is necessary to analyse separately the Australian's front-page stories and its editorial line.

Here is an outline of the stories that appeared on the front page of the Australian between late April and mid-June. It gives some idea of what someone who bought the paper and was interested mainly in the day's most important news would have learned. I apologise to readers for the detail, but without it the astonishing pro-mining company bias of the Australian's coverage of the super profits tax cannot be grasped.

On 24 April the paper reported that "a massive new tax," which mining executives would regard as a "thermo-nuclear option," was in prospect. On 30 April it reported on "the fury" of the miners and the savage likely reduction in their profits of what was called a "double tax." On 3 May it reported that Rudd intended to "milk the mining boom" with his $10 billion tax. On 4 May it reported that Rudd had been accused by the mining industry of not understanding "the real world" and that at least $9 billion had been wiped off the share-market value of mining companies. On 5 May it reported that Rudd was "locked in tense discussions" with mining executives while a further $7 billion of share value was wiped out. On 6 May it reported that in Perth Rudd had been involved in a "bare-knuckle brawl" with thirty of the nation's "most powerful executives" and that Rio Tinto had "shelved" a planned $11 billion investment. On 7 May it reported that "Twiggy" Forrest had claimed that the tax "could jeopardise his multi-billion-dollar expansion plans." It also reported that Santos had deferred for up to six months a decision on whether or not to build a $15 billion LNG export terminal. On 8 May it reported that the miners believed they had been "double-crossed" by the Rudd government. On 11 May it reported that state governments were backing the miners over the tax. On 15 May it reported that four Labor-held seats were in jeopardy because of it. On 18 May it reported that Papua New Guinea was looking forward to new investments being "driven offshore" to it. On 19 May it reported a back-flip affecting the quarry industries. On 20 May it reported that Forrest was now planning to abandon a $17.7 billion iron-ore investment. On 22 May it reported that Rudd had been forced to deny that the tax had caused a drop in the value of the dollar. On 27 May it reported an impending major Rudd government backdown. On 31 May it reported that Rio Tinto regarded the government's advertisements as "misleading." On 1 June, it reported that public opinion was strongly opposed to the mining tax. On 2 June it called on the government to prove its advertising claims were accurate. On 4 June it reported that mining workers were worried about their jobs. On 7 June it reported that the mining tax could lose Labor the next election. On 8 June it reported tensions between trade unions over the tax. On 9 June it reported that the "revered" former Labor minister Peter Walsh was fiercely hostile to the tax and that taxpayers would pay for any future BP-like environmental disaster. On 12 June it reported that the "attempts to make the mining industry a cash cow have challenged international investment in Australia." On 16 June it reported "the first signs" of government compromise and that steel workers now faced "an uncertain future." And on 17 June it reported that mining companies wanted guarantees from the Australian government of the kind they required when operating in "developing and unstable countries."

Between late April and mid-June I discovered only one positive front-page article in the *Australian* on the mining tax. On 17 May Ross Garnaut described it as "elegant." Four days later, however, he was reported as calling on the Rudd government to make changes to it. The conclusion I draw is simple. To judge by its front-page coverage, if the *Australian* had been directly owned by BHP Billiton and Rio Tinto or by the Minerals Council of Australia, it could not have done a better job of killing off the tax.

What then of the *Australian*'s editorial coverage? It is a strange fact that the paper began by supporting the super profits tax suggested to the Rudd government by the head of Treasury, Dr Ken Henry, as part of his major tax-reform report. On 3 May the *Australian* argued that while the resources rent tax, as it was called at that time, would be "controversial" and would draw "complaints from the mining industry," it would "benefit taxpayers and is a courageous policy move." The *Australian* still supported the tax on 15 May – "it makes sense to secure a reasonable price for our finite minerals, and to use mining revenue to address the two-speed economy and cut out boom and bust cycles" – although by now it was worried that Labor had failed to sell its "good story" and allowed "miners' complaints to dominate the news cycle."

Just one day later, it suddenly, indeed stunningly, to use Paul Kelly's favourite word, became a sworn opponent. The mining tax was far too costly for the industry. It might have "an intellectual elegance" about it, but that would appeal only to people who never had "to make a dollar in the real world." The *Australian* announced that it was precisely such people – Kevin Rudd, Julia Gillard, Wayne Swan and Lindsay Tanner – who now had control of the Australian economy. The prime minister was the worst example. He must understand that his job was "less to regulate the market, as he promised to do in his 2009 essay on how government could save capitalism, than to assist industry in expanding the economy." Before mid-May the *Australian* had described the super profits tax as "a courageous policy move." By mid-June it described the tax as "Robin Hood economics." "Robbing mining companies to pay the poor will shrink the nation's wealth if the tax jeopardises investment and the industry that earns a third of our export income." What Rudd now needed was "a quick course on capitalism." On the question of the super profits tax, the front-page reports and the *Australian*'s editorials were by now perfectly aligned.

The mining tax was more than an economic measure for the *Australian*. It was the defining issue by which the prime ministership and the character of Kevin Rudd could be assessed. Faced with an unprecedented mining-company advertising campaign, Rudd let it be known to Peter Hartcher that he felt "the need to demonstrate strength." It needed to be made clear that Australia was run by a democratic government and not by a handful of miners. The *Australian* now exploded. The prime minister was "spoiling for a fight on the resources super-profits tax." According to the paper, this was in part a reflection of his strange personality – one that (unlike Chris Mitchell's) could not accept another's point of view. But it was far more than that. Since the time of Hawke, Labor had worked with business to expand the economy. Rudd was putting that legacy at risk. His anti-business behaviour resembled that of Gough Whitlam "when he decided to take on the miners 35 years ago." "The contrast between the Whitlam–Rudd and Hawke–Keating approaches could not be clearer." As prime minister, Rudd had "emerged as an old-style Labor leader of a kind not seen for more than a generation, more Gough Whitlam heavy than John Howard lite." Remember, in its 27 October 2007 editorial the *Australian* had mocked the daydreaming Left's delusions about Kevin Rudd. Perhaps, it joked, he might turn out to be the best actor ever to walk the Australian political stage, metamorphosing into a Whitlamesque reformer. It had happened! Rudd did not understand that Australians had changed since the time of Whitlam:

> [I]t is the resource super-profits tax that has proved to be the real turning point for modern Australia's enterprise-focused class, crystallising its suspicions that this is a government psychologically out of touch with their aspirations. They get the fact that Mr Rudd does not get them – and now they are threatening to withdraw their support … It is as if the boy from Nambour who is now worth millions

can't accept that his fellow Australians are equally aspirational. Instead he persists in viewing them through the outdated lens of left-wing ideology, class warfare and economic protectionism.

Three days after this editorial Rudd was gone. Chris Mitchell assured both Sally Neighbour and me that he had not wished it so. That was not what his newspaper said. It called the removal of Rudd "the coup we had to have."

At the *Australian* it was now time to gloat. Chris Mitchell was interviewed twice by two of his trusted go-to journalists, Geoff Elliott and Tom Dusevic, about the performance of the *Australian* in reporting the last months of Rudd. The purpose of these articles was to show that compared to the dismal performance of the political reporters who worked for Fairfax and the ABC, only the *Australian* had been penetrating and objective. Elliott turned to the right-wing Sydney talkback radio host Ray Hadley for evidence that it was the Fairfax papers rather than the *Australian* that had an ideological agenda. Hadley obliged: "I wouldn't be surprised if they entered the fray with a leotard and pompoms as cheerleaders for the government. Their objectivity is certainly in question." Tom Dusevic canvassed the opinion of a former Fairfax editor, Steve Harris. He thought both the ABC and Fairfax had become "… self-referential. We think we have got this issue right, they say, and then keeping looking [sic] for evidence to show they are right …" It was their opponents who had an ideological agenda and who were self-referential. It is hard to imagine a clearer example of what psychologists call projection. What is really frightening is that this is what the cult-like inner circle at Chris Mitchell's *Australian* now genuinely believed.

There are two ways of misunderstanding the role that the *Australian* played in the downfall of Kevin Rudd. One way is to exaggerate its influence. Rudd was too politically isolated. His decision to postpone the emissions trading scheme was a very serious mistake. When he decided to tax the miners, he needed far greater support inside his own party.

The other way is to think of the role of the *Australian* as minor. Rudd was not destroyed by the weight of public opinion. On only one occasion, according to Newspoll, was his rating as preferred prime minister lower than 50 per cent. He was destroyed by an internal Labor Party coup. As the *Australian* had now become by far the most important newspaper for the political class, the unrelentingly personal and ideological campaign it waged against Rudd in the months between February and June 2010 undoubtedly helped crystallise opposition to him inside the caucus and the party. In this way the *Australian* was a very important catalyst leading to his fall.

Something else had happened during these months. The *Australian* had become a key player in federal politics and one that had recently tasted blood. The importance of this would become manifest following the August 2010 election, when an alliance formed between Gillard Labor and the Greens.

On 27 September 2010, James Massola, a young member of the *Australian's* Canberra press gallery, published an article called "Controversial political blogger unmasked as a federal public servant." The public servant "unmasked" was Dr Greg Jericho, an employee in the film section of the Department of Environment, Heritage, Water and the Arts, who wrote a left-of-centre blog about politics and sport under the pseudonym of "Grog's Gamut." In a recent speech to the Melbourne Writers' Festival, the chair of the ABC, Mark Scott, had spoken of bringing to the attention of the ABC executive a Grog's Gamut post criticising the mediocre, policy-light performance of the Canberra press gallery in the 2010 election campaign. In his exposé Massola had obviously absorbed the house style of the *Australian*. What appeared to be a straight report was in fact an accusation, mounted by false inference and innuendo. During the home-insulation debacle Jericho had defended his minister, Peter Garrett, in one posting. He had ridiculed Garrett's Shadow, Greg Hunt, and the Opposition leader, Tony Abbott. As he was obviously a partisan ALP supporter, his pseudonymous blogging might well be in breach of "the Public Service code of conduct." In his imposture, Jericho was likened to Helen Demidenko, the Anglo-Australian novelist who had masqueraded as the daughter of a Ukrainian war criminal. In response to the Massola article, Jericho wrote a lucid blog entry defending convincingly both his decision to write pseudonymously and his public-service impartiality. The blog then fell silent while a public-service inquiry into Jericho's behaviour took place. After an uncomfortable fortnight, Jericho's blog resumed, under his real name.

Massola's unmasking of Jericho inspired a flood of tweets. A few people defended Massola. Many criticised him, some fiercely and intemperately. A selection was printed in an article in the *Australian*. One came from Catherine Deveny, who had been sacked as a columnist for the *Age* on the basis of an injudicious tweet. Her contribution to the unmasking question

– "You f**kwit" – was reproduced. Once bitten, twice bold. Massola was defended in an *Australian* editorial: "[L]et's not elevate the right to pursue what amounts to vanity publishing on the net to an issue of freedom of speech." Massola wrote a follow-up article. He argued that Jericho had political influence and that with influence came "political responsibility." As a public servant, especially one expressing partisan views, he had no right to pseudonymity. New accusations were made. According to Massola, Jericho had tweeted as Grog's Gamut during office hours. When he recently attended a "new media" conference, it was unclear whether he was on leave or had cleared his absence from work with his supervisor.

The conference Massola referred to, which both he and Jericho had attended, had been organised by a former ABC journalist and now university lecturer, Julie Posetti. She had invited Jericho to the conference. Posetti was one of Massola's fiercest critics. In one of her tweets, in defending the idea of pseudonymity, she referred to the case of the anti-apartheid hero Steve Biko. Inside the *Australian* her remark was seized upon in the same way David Marr's reference to the rise of Hitler had been twisted during the *Media Watch* affair. Posetti received abusive emails and tweets from journalists at the *Australian*. She was told she was not fit to teach journalism at university. Her supposed analogy between the situations facing Jericho and Biko was nonsensical, hysterical and disgusting. She was also criticised on these grounds, although more temperately, by Geoff Elliott in the pages of the *Australian*.

Posetti hit back on the *Drum*. "In nobody's fantasy, other than a few confused journalists at *The Australian*, was I actually suggesting Steve Biko and 'Grog's Gamut' were 'freedom fighters' of a similar calibre with comparable causes ... That is not to say that Greg Jericho didn't stand to suffer consequences as a result of being outed." Posetti now made some accusations of her own. Several #groggate (as it was now called) tweeters had contacted her. If they were to be believed, "a reporter on *The Australian* had telephoned their employers, asking for strong action to be taken against employees for comments (some using very strong language) directed at James Massola via Twitter." Posetti cited in detail one example of an employee who had received a warning. She argued that the accusations against Jericho – about his breach of the public-service code of ethics; about his attendance at the conference without official permission – were provably false.

The *Australian* had already reported that Jericho had kept his job. It soon reported that he had been permitted to resume his blog under his real name. Now it reprinted an opinion column – "Blogger's unmasking triggers yawn-inducing Murdoch rants" – linking the absurd fuss about Jericho to a disease it called the "Murdoch Derangement Syndrome" – a disease which, as I write these words at the height of the *News of the World* disgrace, seems to have afflicted the entire British nation. At this point, surely, it was reasonable to assume that the Grog's Gamut controversy would be allowed to die. The assumption rests on a misunderstanding of the bullying culture of the *Australian*.

In late November 2010 Julie Posetti attended the annual conference of the Journalism Education Association of Australia. On 25 November Asa Wahlquist spoke briefly on a panel at the conference. She had been the rural reporter for the *Australian*, having recently resigned because of ill health. This in part is what she said:

> Climate change was part of what I covered. It was absolutely excruciating, it was torture, there's no other way to put it. I resigned two months ago and the stress of all that is one of the reasons that led to my resignation ... [M]y editor, my editor-in-chief at the *Australian*, was taking a political view and he's gone down the eco-fascist line, he sees climate change as being a political movement that the Left has now adopted that will, aims to, destroy everything he loves and values ... [O]n a personal level it was just ... it was unbearable, professionally compromising and personally pretty debilitating ... I think that my basic problem was that I always wanted to approach it [climate change] as a science story and I was in a context where

it was seen as a political story instead and as a journalist you have
no power in that situation ... [S]omeone just rewrites your copy,
which happens more than you'd like to know. Plus the other thing
that was happening at the *Australian* before I left was that the editor-
in-chief and the edits [or "editors," the recording at this moment is
unclear] becoming more prescriptive and you saw ... in the lead-up
to the election where you were actually being told what to write ...

As was her custom, Julie Posetti tweeted to her 4500 or so followers during
Asa Wahlquist's talk. "Wahlquist: 'Chris Mitchell (Oz Ed) goes down the
Eco-Fascist line' on #climatechange. 'I left just because I couldn't do it
anymore.'" And: "Wahlquist: 'In the lead up to the election the Ed in
Chief was increasingly telling me what to write.' It was prescriptive."
Posetti suspected that journalists at the *Australian* had been monitoring her
tweets closely since #groggate erupted. Every time she tweeted something critical about the *Australian*, she told me, she received "rapid-fire"
responses from reporters at the paper, some of whom were not followers
of her twitter feed. At the conference these suspicions were confirmed.
Within hours of Posetti's tweets, Wahlquist told the conference organisers
that she had been contacted by Chris Mitchell and asked by a reporter at
the *Australian* whether Posetti's tweets were accurate. Mitchell had sent an
email entitled "defamation" threatening: "If I do not have an apology in
writing from you today you will see me in court. I promise, Chris." That
very afternoon, Wahlquist said: "Those 'tweets' were inaccurate and
taken out of context ... I would like to place on record that I have never
had a conversation with the Editor-in-Chief of the *Australian* about climate
change. In fact I have not had a conversation with Mr Mitchell on any
subject for many years."

On the following day Mitchell let it be known that he intended to sue
not Asa Wahlquist but Julie Posetti for defamation. He told me in our
interview that he did so to teach her and others a much-needed lesson
about the law and the ethics of journalism. Posetti was unable to sleep for

several days. Her anxiety lifted a little when a recording of the Wahlquist talk appeared. It showed that her tweets were in essence accurate, a point that in the online edition of the *Australian* Caroline Overington soon conceded. On 29 November Posetti nonetheless received a letter from the solicitors at Blake Dawson threatening defamation action unless she offered an immediate apology. Mitchell offered "mediation" and invited Posetti to the offices of the *Australian* to assess the openness and accountability of the editorial process. He supported this action with the article by Graham Lloyd discussed earlier in this essay, defending his paper's coverage of climate change, and an article by Geoff Elliott entitled "Defamation case a timely reminder of the risks of hateful tweeting."

With the strong backing of her vice chancellor at the University of Canberra, Stephen Parker, and with a deluge of support, some coming secretly from reporters at the *Australian* and other News Limited papers, Posetti was determined not to cave in. She had courage. A letter was sent on her behalf by H.W.L. Ebsworth Lawyers on 9 December declining to apologise for what had already been acknowledged by the *Australian* to have been accurate tweets. Posetti would accept the invitation to observe the daily conference at the *Australian* on the condition that the editor-in-chief was willing to attend some of her university lectures. She received no response. There the matter rested.

Pressure, however, was maintained. Posetti knew that her tweets and public appearances were still being closely monitored. In early May 2011 she spoke to Deborah Cameron about Twitter on ABC radio in Sydney. Caroline Overington contacted her at once. Why had she not acknowledged in the interview that she was involved in a legal dispute with the *Australian*? "We have a transcript of your comments." On 5 May 2011, criticism of Posetti's alleged omission appeared in the *Australian*. The following day a correction appeared. A comment of Cameron's had been attributed to Posetti. On 7 May Overington began tweeting on the Posetti matter: "julie's best bet is to say: i should have called chris mitchell for a response. next time I will"; "actually, i'm trying to help because I reckon julie's caught in a rough trap, but together we could spring it"; "oh, please. he's not even in the country, let alone at my elbow"; "yes, I do think it will proceed to court, it was ugly what was said about him. and false."

In the case of defamation, writs must be issued within one year. At the time of writing a writ had not yet been issued. Even though Chris Mitchell told me in our interview that he was unlikely to proceed, the threat had not been withdrawn.

As so often with the *Australian*, a challenge from someone who would not be intimidated had been transformed into a test of strength between radically unequal partners. Readers can make of this story what they will. For my part I am astonished that an editor of a major daily newspaper who has millions of words at his disposal and whose newspaper tears flesh off people every day, and who is on record as saying that the defamation laws are a blight on freedom of expression in Australia, should think it reasonable to threaten to sue a young university lecturer over what were essentially two accurate tweets of someone else's conference talk.

*

Milan Kundera's first novel is called *The Joke*. It begins in 1950s communist Czechoslovakia. In an impish mood, Ludvik sends a postcard to his girl-friend: "Optimism is the opium of the people! A healthy atmosphere stinks of stupidity! Long live Trotsky!" Ludvik is expelled from the Communist Party and sent to work down a mine as part of a labour brigade. When thinking about the case of Larissa Behrendt, this novel I read more than forty years ago came to mind. (Before you repair to your keyboards, Caroline, Geoff, Patricia, no, I am not suggesting an analogy between Gottwald's Czechoslovakia and Mitchell's *Australian*.)

Late in the evening on Monday, 11 April 2011, the 42-year-old professor Larissa Behrendt, research director of the Jumbunna Centre at the University of Technology, Sydney, was watching an episode of the raw and violent American television series *Deadwood* on ABC 2 with her partner, Michael

Lavarch, a former attorney-general in the Keating government. At the same time *Q&A* was screening on ABC 1. One of the panellists was the Warlpiri woman from Alice Springs Bess Price. Price is a science graduate, a businesswoman and a politically committed activist sympathetic to the assimilationist group known as the Bennelong Society, whose president is Gary Johns, for whose book, mentioned earlier in this essay, Bess Price wrote the foreword. She is also a strong supporter of the federal government's Northern Territory Intervention.

Nothing divides the Australian indigenous community more deeply than the Intervention. As mentioned earlier in this essay, some leading Aboriginal intellectuals – like Noel Pearson and Marcia Langton – are strong supporters. Others – like Pat and Mick Dodson and Larissa Behrendt – are strong opponents. Nor is this divide any less deep among indigenous people living under the Intervention. Some obviously do support it. The evidence, however, would suggest that more of those living under it are now opposed. In the 2007 election, following the Howard government's decision to act, in the heavily Aboriginal seat of Lingiari in the Northern Territory there was a 3.7 per cent swing against the Country–Liberal Party candidate. In the 2010 election, following the Rudd government's decision to continue the Intervention, there was a 13.9 per cent swing against the Labor candidate. All of it went either to two independents or to the Greens candidate, Barb Shaw, an anti-Intervention activist.

While Behrendt was watching *Deadwood*, many of her friends were watching *Q&A*. There were very many hostile tweets. One came from the indigenous radio presenter Rhianna Patrick. On *Deadwood* there had just been a characteristic scene. Larissa tweeted in response to something from her friend Rhianna: "I watched a show where a guy had sex with a horse and I'm sure it was less offensive than Bess Price." It was a bad joke; a sour joke; a joke with a political sting. But it was a joke. Old human instincts often do not keep up with technology. Many people tweet to friends forgetting that what they say is public and not private. I am almost certain this was the case here.

The *Australian* on 14 April had a prominent front-page story about the tweet. The author was one of the team of reporters on indigenous affairs, Patricia Karvelas. Behrendt knew of her mainly as the journalist who had attacked Mick Dodson some years earlier. Dodson was opposed to freehold title on Aboriginal reserves. Karvelas had pointed out that Dodson, who held a chair at the Australian National University, owned a house in Canberra. Ergo, he was a hypocrite. Her article was illustrated with a photograph of his house. Karvelas' article on Behrendt was entitled "More offensive than 'sex with a horse': Behrendt's Twitter slur against black leader." Karvelas provided a brief account of Behrendt's explanation of the tweet. She quoted Price at greater length. Behrendt was at the time involved with other lighter-skinned Aborigines in a case against Andrew Bolt, who had accused such people of using their ancestry for personal profit. Price claimed: "This is worse than what she is accusing Bolt of." She was seeking legal advice. Price also claimed that as an urban indigenous academic Behrendt was "out of touch" with central Australian Aborigines. Price wanted for her children what Behrendt already had. She called Behrendt a "white blackfella." She claimed the group of white blackfellas wanted to "control" bush people and rob them of their voice. Their culture and hers were entirely different. On 14 April Karvelas' article was accompanied by an anti-Behrendt opinion column from Gary Johns. Johns labelled Behrendt "a gross hypocrite" regarding her legal case against Bolt. What she tweeted about Price was far more offensive than anything Bolt had written about light-skinned Aborigines. For Johns, the worst examples of racism in the past twenty years in Australia were the attacks unleashed against whites during the inquiries into Aboriginal deaths in custody and Aboriginal child removal. He expressed the hope that UTS would "review" Behrendt's position and those of everyone employed at the Jumbunna Centre holding "similarly prejudicial views."

By now Behrendt was badly shaken and regretful. She did not know Bess Price. She had meant her no offence. She decided to make a public apology, which she sent both to the *Australian* and the *Sydney Morning Herald*.

"I take full responsibility for my carelessness in the way I expressed myself and I apologise to Ms Price unreservedly." Not surprisingly, it was not run by the *Herald*. No paper in the country other than the *Australian* thought an injudicious late-night tweet newsworthy, let alone worthy of prominent front-page treatment. Behrendt also sent Bess Price a personal apology by email: "Dear Ms Price, I very much regret that a recent tweet of mine has caused you deep offence. I unreservedly offer you a heartfelt apology for that and hope you can accept it. Sincerely, Larissa."

Behrendt's apologies were reported on the front page of the *Australian* on 15 April. Karvelas was, however, a master of the *Australian*'s familiar false-inference, disguised-assumption, report-as-accusation house style. As she wrote: "The high-profile indigenous lawyer was yesterday forced into a humiliating apology to Ms Price, an Aboriginal woman who supports the federal intervention in Northern Territory communities, after indigenous leaders expressed outrage at the comment." This sentence suggested that Behrendt was insincere. She had been forced to apologise. It described the apology not as welcome but "humiliating." It suggested that Aboriginal leaders were all "outraged" at Behrendt. In fact, many in the Territory, like Barb Shaw and Marlene Hodder, were outraged not at Larissa Behrendt's tweet but at Bess Price's *Q&A* claim that almost all indigenous women in the Territory supported the Intervention. The sentence finally implied that as "a high-profile lawyer" she had no idea about what was happening in Bess Price's "real" world.

Karvelas' 15 April article was accompanied by an editorial, "Who tweets for Aborigines?" In it Behrendt's apology was not humiliating but "belated." The editorial explained the significance of the affair like this: "The Twitter exchanges reveal the split between urban and remote Aboriginal leaders over Canberra's intervention in dysfunctional communities … the professional class of urban blacks" was more interested in "gesture politics and symbolism" than in "the shameful conditions endured by many Aborigines." Five letters were published, all extremely hostile to Behrendt. On the page alongside the editorial and the letters, there appeared a furious anti-Behrendt opinion column – "Aboriginal sophisticates undermine bush sisters" – by the indigenous academic Marcia Langton. It gave eloquent expression to the false binary opposition that dominated the *Australian*'s anti-Behrendt campaign – privileged, ivory-tower urban anti-Intervention Aborigines versus unprivileged pro-Intervention Aborigines on the ground. This binary was based on the self-evidently inaccurate proposition that indigenous people in the Territory overwhelmingly favoured the Intervention. Langton supported this by claiming that Bess Price lived in Yuendumu. In fact she had not lived there for twenty years. Langton called the twitter message "foul." She argued that never in her life had she witnessed such disrespect for an elder except when people were under the influence of drugs or alcohol. She claimed that it was Bess Price's "plea for an inquiry into the culture of sexual abuse" that Behrendt had found "offensive." This was untrue and obviously damaging. She disparaged Behrendt as someone who had not been "brought up in the Aboriginal way." She called Behrendt and her friends "sepia-toned Sydney activists." She wondered whether or not Bolt was right after all about such people. Langton even compared Behrendt and those like her to white patrol officers who thought they knew better than the "natives" what to think.

Marcia Langton's central accusation – from which everything else flowed – was entirely false. Larissa Behrendt was not an out-of-touch academic. She had worked for years with people in the remote areas of north-west New South Wales, Wilcannia, Menindee and Lightning Ridge, but also throughout the communities in the Northern Territory and the town camps round Alice Springs, travelling there regularly, almost every year. After the Bess Price controversy erupted, Valerie Martin Napaljarri wrote these words in her support: "I am a Warlpiri woman and community spokesperson from Yuendumu. I also spend time living in Kalkaringi … Larissa is very highly respected by me and others in my community. I have worked closely with her advocating for our rights. In 2010 I travelled with her out to community of Ampilatwatja to participate in meetings. She was always very respectful and spoke just what we were feeling."

When I spoke to her, Larissa Behrendt was still very deeply upset by Marcia Langton's column. It hurt her far more than attacks by people like Keith Windschuttle. Langton's hostility began in 2008, in an article in the *Griffith Review*, once it was clear that Behrendt and Langton differed over the Intervention. Behrendt contrasted Langton's personal denigration with Noel Pearson's respectful style of intellectual disagreement. She refused, however, to withdraw her admiration from Langton, whom she had always looked upon as a courageous role model for younger indigenous women like herself. Ideological differences would never affect that.

The *Australian* had devoted two front-page stories, two opinion columns and an editorial to Larissa Behrendt's late-night tweet, which shortly and without irony the *Australian*'s gossip columnist called "the slur of the century." Behrendt had issued two unqualified apologies. Surely now the affair was over.

In fact it had hardly begun. On 16 April Patricia Karvelas reported that "pressure was mounting" for Behrendt to be dismissed from her role as head of the Gillard government's inquiry into indigenous higher education. In the culture of the *Australian*, "pressure is mounting" is code for a journalist phoning people whose views are well known to elicit a predictable comment supporting the story that is about to be run. In this instance Karvelas appears to have phoned three indigenous leaders, Sue Gordon, Warren Mundine and Alison Anderson, all of whom were supportive of the Intervention and hostile to the Left. They were of the opinion that Behrendt was not a suitable person to lead the government inquiry. So was the spokesperson for the Country–Liberals in the Northern Territory, Adam Giles. For the first time, there was recognition that not everyone was of identical mind. Late in the article, Barb Shaw was quoted, expressing confidence in Behrendt and outrage at Bess Price's misrepresentation of indigenous feeling about the Intervention in the town camps and Aboriginal communities of the Territory. This was countered by Bess

Price's husband. He said that she had been overwhelmed by "a tsunami of support." Karvelas' report was followed by yet another opinion piece, a 1350-word attack on Behrendt by the cultural warrior and editorial writer at the *Australian* Chris Kenny, and by four more hostile letters to the editor.

On 18 April the campaign changed direction. In another front-page story – "Uni report adds to scrutiny on Behrendt" – Patricia Karvelas reported that Behrendt's suitability as head of the Gillard government's inquiry into indigenous higher education had been called into question "in the wake of a highly critical assessment of indigenous education at the University of Technology Sydney." Its "revelation" would "put more pressure on Labor to choose a new head for its indigenous higher education review." Karvelas had been sent a report into the Faculty of Arts and Social Sciences. The report suggested problems with its indigenous program. As Karvelas conceded, Behrendt was not mentioned in the report and the Jumbunna Centre was not located in the arts faculty. She reported, however, that "some submissions ... criticised Jumbunna for focusing more on research than its role in providing student services." What she did not report was that Larissa Behrendt was not the head of the Jumbunna Centre but its research director, whose role was to direct its research program and win research grants. It seems surpassingly strange that she was criticised for doing her job well. This line of attack was purest moonshine. It was not pursued.

Karvelas was not yet done. On 19 April readers learnt that "Behrendt 'sought ban on writer.'" An indigenous human-rights lawyer from Perth, Hannah McGlade, had contacted the *Australian*. She claimed Behrendt had tried to stop her writing a column for the *National Indigenous Times*. "'It was me or her, apparently,' Ms McGlade said." The present editor of the NIT, Stephen Hagan, confirmed McGlade's story. Both Behrendt and Chris Graham, its former editor, denied that this was an even remotely accurate version of what had occurred. The following day Karvelas published "a leaked email" which, she claimed, "demonstrates [Behrendt] did indeed try to have another Aboriginal woman banned from writing for *The*

National Indigenous Times." It did no such thing. At the time of the incident Larissa Behrendt was not writing her column for the NIT. Recently the editorship had changed hands. When she learned that Hannah McGlade was going to be a columnist, Behrendt was upset. She felt that McGlade had displayed irrational animosity to her in the past. She felt uncomfortable about resuming her column under a new editor alongside someone as hostile as McGlade. Behrendt decided to discuss the situation with one of the owners of the paper, Beverley Wyner. Wyner told her that she would ask Stephen Hagan to ring so they could discuss the problem. No phone call came. Instead, in the next issue of the NIT, Behrendt read that her column had been terminated. It was at this point that she wrote the email that had been leaked to Karvelas. In Karvelas' article the critical line in the email reads: "Then I read the editorial in the paper when it came out and realised that my time with NIT had come to an end." Karvelas adds this note: "The editorial announces McGlade as one of the paper's permanent columnists." The clear suggestion here is that Behrendt had tried to have McGlade banned and had failed. It was the other way round. Behrendt had been a long-time NIT contributor. She had been paid a pittance or not at all. Now, without the courtesy of the promised phone conversation with Hagan concerning the discomfort she felt about having someone as hostile to her as Hannah McGlade as a fellow columnist, Behrendt had read in the editorial that she had been sacked.

By now an image of Behrendt had taken shape. She was a privileged ivory-tower indigenous academic unaware of and indifferent to the plight of Aborigines living in the remote communities. She had written a monstrous tweet, which had been published on eight occasions in the *Australian*. Her apologies had been both belated and humiliating. She was unfit to lead the inquiry into indigenous higher education. She had let the indigenous students at UTS down. She had tried to have a fellow female Aboriginal lawyer banned. Larissa Behrendt felt as if she was experiencing a never-ending nightmare. Close friends and family advised her to take a holiday to get away. At four o'clock each afternoon she was sick to the stomach, dreading new charges from Patricia Karvelas. Surely there could be no more.

In some ways the worst calumny was still to come. Larissa Behrendt came from an unprivileged background, with a white mother and an indigenous father whose mother had been brought up in an institution after her own mother died. She had graduated in law from the University of New South Wales and had been awarded a scholarship to do perhaps the most prestigious law degree in the English-speaking world, the Master of Laws at Harvard. Behrendt had not only completed the Masters successfully, she was one of only twelve students in her year admitted to the degree of Doctor of Jurisprudence. She completed the doctorate in three years rather than the more usual four. On 21 April, the same day that the "Strewth" columnist Graeme Leech called her tweet "the slur of the century," the *Australian* published an article by Keith Windschuttle which suggested that her scholarship to Harvard and the degrees she was awarded there had not been earned. Behrendt had been assisted in her Harvard application by Bobbi Sykes. But there were questions about Bobbi Sykes' Aboriginality. Therefore … it was unclear exactly what. The suggestion that she did not deserve her scholarship to Harvard was a slur on an unnamed Australian authority. The suggestion that she did not deserve her doctorate was a slur on Harvard University. All this was truly foul. Oddly enough, shortly after I interviewed Larissa Behrendt she received the following letter from one of the most distinguished international lawyers, Martha Minow, the Jeremiah Smith, Jr Professor of Law at Harvard. "I send congratulations on your recognition for your advocacy for the rights of Aboriginal and Torres Straits Islanders. I wanted you to know how delighted we are to see a graduate of this place make such a difference."

Before this letter arrived, there was still more to come. On 23 April the *Australian* published another characteristically stream-of-consciousness editorial complaining about Larissa Behrendt's tweet, "the moralising mumbo-jumbo spreading like a virus from university humanities departments" and "another failed experiment, an online opinion forum known as *Crikey*." On 28 April it published an article about a supposedly anti-Behrendt petition circulating in the Northern Territory signed by 121 Warlpiri people and additional petitions "said to be signed" by 800 more people. I have seen a copy of the Warlpiri petition in defence of Bess Price. It attacks Barb Shaw and Marlene Hodder. It does not mention Larissa Behrendt. Finally, on 2 June the *Australian* published a report – "'Divisive' academic paid \$641 daily fee" – which suggested that Larissa Behrendt was doing very well indeed out of her role as head of the Gillard government's inquiry into higher education. This was yet another lie. The consultancy fee is paid directly to her university. Behrendt does not benefit by one cent.

In the whole disgraceful saga of protracted character assassination, the only decent article in the *Australian* was written by Noel Pearson. He made it clear that he completely disagreed with Behrendt's anti-Intervention ideas. But he also made it clear that her achievements ought to be an inspiration to young indigenous people. He had previously urged the government to appoint Behrendt to the indigenous committee inquiring into the promised constitutional referendum. He now suggested that she was the right person to lead the inquiry into indigenous higher education.

On 15 June I interviewed Chris Mitchell and Paul Kelly. Both believed the articles on Larissa Behrendt were what she deserved. To my surprise Kelly was even more vehement than Mitchell. Following this I met Larissa Behrendt. In the course of the interview I asked her to comment on the impact the *Australian*'s campaign had had upon her life. She could not speak. We quickly passed on to other questions.

THE GREENS: "THEY ARE HYPOCRITES; THEY ARE BAD FOR THE NATION; AND THEY SHOULD BE DESTROYED AT THE BALLOT BOX"

Isaiah Berlin once argued that thinkers could be divided into two types: foxes and hedgehogs. Foxes knew many small things. Hedgehogs knew one big thing. It is also possible to apply Berlin's notion to political leaders. Senator Bob Brown has led the Greens Party for decades. He knows one big thing – namely, that as a consequence of global warming the future of the earth is at risk. Because this understanding has gradually deepened, especially among the better-educated sections of the Australian population, many of whom now regard the issue of climate change as incomparably the most important political issue of contemporary times, and because Bob Brown is known to be principled and unwavering on this question, support for his party has steadily grown. This view is not shared by the editor-in-chief of the *Australian*. He has long despised the Greens. So has Rupert Murdoch. When he visited Australia in late 2010, he spoke of this country as "a wonderful land of opportunity" and warned: "Whatever you do, don't let the bloody Greens mess it up."

On 21 August 2010, there was an Australian federal election. Neither the Labor Party nor the Coalition won a majority. Four independents were elected whose votes would determine who formed government. The most significant outcome of the election, however, was the increase in the vote for the Greens. The party received 11.7 per cent, or one and a half million, of the votes for the House of Representatives. One Greens member, Adam Bandt, was elected to the lower house. Six Greens Senators were elected. This meant that when the new Senate assembled on 1 July 2011, there would be nine Greens members who would now hold the balance of power, that is to say would determine the outcome of any legislation where Labor and the Coalition disagreed. Not only was this by far the best result the Greens had ever achieved, it was also the best result at any federal election achieved by any so-called third party.

For eighteen days it was unclear whether the four independents would support a Labor or a Coalition government. The *Australian* clearly hoped that the independents, three of whom held country seats, would support the Coalition. There were many ways of trying to influence their decision. One was to launch a propaganda war against the Greens. In preparation for this essay I spoke to Bob Brown. He told me that despite its very long-standing hostility, he noticed from the day after the election an obvious change of mood and level of aggression among the journalists from the *Australian*, who dominated the Canberra press gallery.

The nature of the unceasing propaganda war waged by the *Australian* – which began on 21 August 2010 and has continued to the present day – needs to be documented in some detail. My analysis will begin with the whole-of-paper coverage of the Greens – news reports, opinion columns, editorials – for the eighteen days between the federal election and the creation of the second Gillard government.

On election day, in separate reports, the *Australian* told its readers that the stock market's "worst fears" were "a hung parliament followed closely by an ALP-controlled lower house and Greens-controlled Senate"; that business "executives" would "go to the polling booth" feeling "very worried about the idea of Greens leader Bob Brown holding the next government to ransom"; and that as Bob Brown planned to retire at the end of his current term, troubles loomed between Senator Christine Milne and the New South Wales Greens candidate, Lee Rhiannon, who would become the favoured target of the *Australian* over the coming months, if she were to be elected. These themes were taken up on the Monday following the election. Readers now learned that business believed that the expected hung parliament and the Greens' position in the Senate spelt the end of prospects for "vital economic reform" and that Lee Rhiannon, who from now on was associated with the so-called watermelon faction of the party – green on the outside; red on the inside – "has had to fend off suggestions she is positioning herself to lead the Greens when Senator Brown, 65, retires." In the *Australian's* by now conventional language, "having to fend off suggestions" is code for denying an untruth put to a target by a journalist from the *Australian*.

On 25 August the *Australian* published its first editorial on the significance of the Greens' outstanding election performance. The editorial ridiculed the claim that the election had witnessed the "real birth of a new political movement." "Political observers who didn't come down in the last shower" had "heard it all before." The success of the Greens was likely to prove ephemeral unless they abandoned their "tomato Left economics." For the one-thousandth time, the Labor Party was warned not to "lurch to the Left." For their part, the Greens were advised to "occupy the ground between the major parties" so as not to "stray from the values of their voters." The ideas that the Greens – the most important left-wing party in Australian history – should try to squeeze into the almost non-existent political space between Labor and the Coalition, and that their voters had supported them without noticing that they were a party of the Left, were, even by the standards of the *Australian*, seriously strange. Obviously the political situation was creating confusion among senior staff there. On the following day the *Australian* ran a comment on its front page by Dennis Shanahan. A day after his paper had advised the Greens to position themselves to the right of Labor, Shanahan described the party in the kind of language B.A. Santamaria might have used about the Communist Party half a century ago. "Bandt is a member of a party that has a worldwide movement, a national structure, funding from overseas and a platform opposed to much of Labor's election policy." Shanahan called for a new election five days after the last. It seemed to Bob Brown as if the *Australian* regarded the result of an election signalling the possibility of a Labor–Greens alliance as somehow illegitimate. Brown interpreted the publication of Shanahan's article as a portent of the virulent anti-Greens campaign to come. He was not wrong.

On 28 August the *Australian* gave prominence in both a report and an extract reproduced in "Cut and Paste" to something Adam Bandt had written fifteen years ago while a Marxist student radical at Monash University, which described the Greens as a "bourgeois party." Bob Brown was asked whether, in the light of this, he still had confidence in the new member for Melbourne. Brown offered Bandt his "160 per cent support." "We are not into book burning in Australia." Perhaps not, although one might have begun to wonder after reading a column that day by Terry McCrann, one of the most senior, influential and rabid members of Rupert Murdoch's Australian stable. McCrann's interpretation of the election was apocalyptic. For him it marked the end of the great period of economic reform begun under John Howard in 1979 and the beginning of a new era where "a permanent Green minority ... will endorse irrational policies from a Labor government and frustrate rational ones from a Coalition one." According to McCrann, Treasury was already under the control of enemy forces – "green most strikingly in its analysis of climate change" and "red in its support for even a 99 per cent super-profits tax." McCrann used the Cold War language of conquest by the Totalitarian Enemy. The Treasury had been "colonised." The Greens had "seized" the balance of power in the Senate. Seized? On 30 August the totalitarian theme took off. A report on the New South Wales Senator-elect Lee Rhiannon, who had foolishly tried to hide her long-distant pro-Soviet past, was headlined: "Forget about Stalinism, I'm a true-blue Green." Not so fast, Lee. On the basis of information from an obscure South Australian Greens party member, Christian Kerr informed readers that in New South Wales the Greens branch was under communist control and that throughout Australia the party consisted of "a small communist core and a great mass of politically naïve people." In his customary world-weary style, David Burchell disagreed about this naivety. He described the party's "grassroots" as consisting of "the foul-smelling detritus from a hundred leftist fragments of yesteryear."

On 1 September Labor and the Greens signed a very significant alliance agreement, which may come to be seen as a turning point in Australian politics. The prime minister committed to meeting regularly with Bob Brown and Adam Bandt. Greens' legislative proposals would be assessed by the prime minister's office and costed by Treasury. The government promised a referendum recognising the indigenous people in the constitution. Perhaps most importantly, it promised to establish a parliamentary committee to investigate how to put a price on carbon. At the time of the alliance agreement, the vital decision of the independents was looming. The *Australian*'s war against the Greens now went into overdrive.

On 2 September no fewer than six articles hostile to the Greens were published. On the front page of the paper readers learned that "Labor's alliance with the Greens" had "sent shock waves through Australia's mining heartland" and that, in the opinion of Paul Kelly, "the once great Labor Party passes into history with this deal." Inside the paper they learned that Australia's "mining chiefs" had voiced their "strong concerns" about the possibility of a "more punitive mining tax and the potential demolition of Australia's coal and uranium industries"; that the alliance "would slug regional areas, place miners' jobs at risk and usher in bans on recreational fishing and a softer policy on boat people"; and that the alliance would revive "the confiscatory attitudes towards reward for effort of the quaint old Left," which included something neither quaint nor old, the "so-called Tobin tax," a levy of one-hundredth of one per cent on all financial transactions. If the prospect of a Tobin tax and the end of recreational fishing was not worry enough, readers learnt that Adam Bandt had been "sleeping with the enemy." This turned out to mean that his partner was an ALP staffer.

And so it went. Between 3 and 7 September there were a dozen articles flaying the Greens. Readers learnt that the Greens' tax policy "was devised by a party that is green with envy" and that their pledge to spend more on dental health would place unwelcome pressure on the budget bottom line. They learned that Origin Energy was concerned about the new power of the Greens; that the coal-seam gas industry had "slammed" the Greens for their "hypocrisy"; that Anna Bligh thought they had "a blinkered view" of the liquefied natural gas industry; and that, surprise, surprise, the chief executives of BHP Billiton, Rio Tinto and Xtrata were "deeply troubled" by the arrival of "Bob Brown's Greens to the Government benches."

As Matthew Stevens helpfully pointed out, "Who can blame them?" The mining executives were indeed, it soon turned out, so troubled by the Labor–Greens alliance that they felt obliged to warn the *Australian* that, sadly enough, they might be compelled to mount yet another advertising campaign against the government. Nor was the danger the Labor–Greens alliance posed to Australia purely economic. Patricia Karvelas, a left-leaning gay feminist according to Chris Mitchell, reported on the front page about the danger of the Greens rushing a "same sex" marriage bill through the parliament by use of a "conscience vote." Russell Trood pointed out that the Greens were about "to become a powerful and malign influence on Labor foreign policy." Although they had led the Gillard government to the promise of a referendum on indigenous constitutional recognition, Wesley Aird was of the view that "as far as indigenous affairs goes, Labor should have nothing to do with the Greens." This was not only Aird's view. On 7 September, as the moment of the decision of the independents approached, Karvelas reported, once more on the front page, "an extraordinary last-minute intervention" from Noel Pearson, appealing to Rob Oakeshott to support the true friend of indigenous Australians, Tony Abbott.

The campaign waged against the Greens in the eighteen days between the 21 August election and the 7 September announcement of the independents' decision for Gillard was so unrelenting, so exaggerated, so obvious, so desperately unbalanced and unfair, that reading through the relevant articles is a comical experience. Bob Brown, however, was not amused. He complained on the ABC's *Lateline* about the astonishing bias shown by the *Australian* in its attempt to wreck the Labor–Greens alliance. Usually the *Australian* denies such accusations with persiflage and Jesuitical nonsense. On this occasion, uncharacteristically, it did not. In its editorial of 7 September the *Australian* argued: "Greens leader Bob Brown has accused *The Australian* of trying to wreck the alliance between the Greens and Labor. We wear Senator Brown's criticism with pride. We believe that he and his Green colleagues are hypocrites; that they are bad for the nation; and that they should be destroyed at the ballot box."

With this statement the *Australian* had ceased even to pretend to be, in the words of its US Murdoch cousin, the execrable Fox News, "fair and balanced." With this statement it made explicit what was already entirely obvious, namely that the *Australian* saw itself not as a mere newspaper, but as a player in the game of national politics, calling upon the vast resources of the Murdoch empire and the millions of words it had available to it to try to influence the national political agenda and to make and unmake governments. The pretence of the *Australian* was that it scrutinised those in power. The reality was that it exercised extraordinary power without either responsibility or accountability. The *Australian's* editorial of 7 September was a perhaps unique and most likely inadvertent moment of honesty.

The Greens took their complaint about the *Australian's* bias to *Media Watch*, which was temporarily in the hands of Paul Barry. In the program of 13 September, Barry reported a statement of Bob Brown to Laura Tingle of the *Australian Financial Review*: "[The paper] sees itself as a determinant of democracy in Australia … It's slipped the role of the fourth estate … and it needs to be taken on." Barry quoted a bizarre sentence from Chris Mitchell in response: "Just as *The Australian* refused to be intimidated by Mr Rudd last year, we have no intention of bowing to Bob Brown's bullying this year." Barry quipped: "Bob Brown's bullying. You've got to be kidding." He did not, however, point out the psychological clue embedded in this line. When faced with opposition of any kind, Mitchell does truly feel himself to be the victim. In the course of our interview he told me, with an apparently straight face, that I was a more powerful voice in the culture wars than he.

Readers of this essay will not be surprised to discover that it was Geoff Elliott whom Mitchell chose for the job of replying to *Media Watch*. Elliott found two impartial sources – the Channel Nine network's director of news and current affairs, Mark Calvert, and Michael Gawenda of the University of Melbourne – to assess the quality of the *Australian's* coverage of the Greens. Neither had any criticism. According to Calvert, "Backing a party, policies and politicians as well as criticising them is healthy for a free press." As was the custom, Mitchell was himself quoted. Bob Brown had complained about twenty hostile articles since 15 August. Of the hundreds of political articles published in the *Australian* since that time, "twenty negatives on the Greens seems very few." "We would have run many more negative stories about Labor and the Coalition in that period." The suggestion here that the *Australian* was not more hostile to the Greens than it was to the Coalition or Labor was both risible and unnecessary. Yet that was what Mitchell apparently wanted his readers to believe.

Shortly after *Media Watch* Mitchell hired an "independent firm," Media Monitors, to probe the question of anti-Greens bias at the *Australian*. Media Monitors found the *Australian*'s coverage of the Greens only "slightly unfavourable." I conducted my own study. I found that in the month following the election the paper published fifty articles on the Greens that were hostile and one that was friendly. In January 2011 the Greens decided on another research tack in the attempt to prove the bleeding obvious. Bob Brown asked the Commonwealth parliamentary library, one of the most scrupulous and professional research bodies in the country, to make an assessment of the impartiality of the *Australian*'s editorials which referred to the Greens in the period between January 2000 and January 2011. The library found five that were positive and 188 that were negative. Of the positive references it said: "Even then these were not glowing endorsements but rather simple agreement with a statement that they had made." For my own part, in preparing for this essay, I read hundreds of randomly selected articles in the *Australian* about the Greens – news reports, opinion columns, editorials – in the year from July 2010 to July 2011. Fewer than ten were positive. Encountering a friendly article on the Greens in the *Australian* was almost as uncommon an experience as discovering a positive reference to the Communist Party of Australia in B.A. Santamaria's *News Weekly* or to the presidency of George W. Bush in *Green Left Weekly*.

After an attentive reading of the opinions of its columnists and its editorials in the months following the election, the following is what an uncritical reader of the *Australian* would have been led to believe. The Greens were a "pernicious and extreme" political movement (Sheridan) with a profound hostility not only to capitalism and the idea of economic growth but also to "the core values of Western civilisation," at whose heart there lurked a new form of totalitarian politics, "coercive utopianism" (Albrecht-sen). Perhaps the political evil they represented went even deeper than this. In Gary Johns' view, they were in essence anti-human, a party that would "never defend humanity against nature," whose leader regarded humans as mere "inhabitants of the earth, along with plants and animals." From the ideological point of view, the Greens were divided between radical conser-vationists and sinister socialists, the watermelon faction as it were. Eventu-ally a showdown between these different tendencies seemed certain to occur, especially after the supposedly imminent retirement of Bob Brown. Greg Sheridan thought of the Greens as "basically the old Socialist Left" of the 1960s Labor Party reborn. For his part Senator Ron Boswell, who wrote on this matter twice, thought of Bob Brown as the left-wing equivalent of Pauline Hanson. His party posed the same kind of threat to Labor as One Nation had once posed to the Coalition. Because the Greens were highly critical of Israel, and because parts of its New South Wales branch supported an economic boycott, something which, incidentally, Bob Brown publicly opposed, both Boswell and Barry Cohen declared in the pages of the *Australian* that the Greens were a straightforwardly "anti-Semitic" party. Almost equally sinister for some of the *Australian*'s columnists was the determination of the Greens to impose their radical social agenda – most importantly legalised euthanasia and same-sex marriage – on their Labor allies and on the nation. Christopher Pearson was particularly exercised about the prospect of same-sex marriage, which he interpreted as in part a subtle Greens' ploy "to reduce the population and drive down national fertility." Presumably Pearson believed that without legalised same-sex marriage gay men and women would simply settle down and have babies.

In the *Australian*'s political analysis of the Labor–Greens alliance, as remarkable as the systematic denigration was the wild exaggeration of the influence the Greens were thought to exert over Labor. An editorial claimed that the Greens now held Labor in their "joyless embrace." Paul Kelly, who was astonished that the Gillard government had signed off on the 1 September agreement with the Greens, thought they were very successfully "playing with Labor's head." As the overwhelming proportion of Greens' preferences was certain to flow to Labor no matter how the Gillard government behaved, the prime minister's capitulation to the Greens was altogether unnecessary and really rather "sad." Neither Hawke nor Keating would have done anything quite so foolish. The most influential journalists and columnists at the *Australian* not only exaggerated the Greens' power. With the singular exception of Graham Richardson, who argued that Bob Brown's success as a leader rested on his remarkable good humour, humility and lack of malice, they also comprehensively misread his political character. Time and again Bob Brown was portrayed as "cunning," "opportunistic" and – this was the favoured description – "hypocritical." It was as if, confronted by a straightforwardly principled politician, the senior journalists at the *Australian* were all nonplussed.

According to the *Australian* the Greens were the party of well-heeled, university-educated, inner-city professionals – teachers, academics, media workers and so on – who had no connection with either the productive parts of the economy or with the life of the suburban "mainstream." The tragedy for Labor was that its alliance with the Greens and its interest in their "boutique issues" – like climate change and same-sex marriage – meant that it was in grave danger of losing touch with the concerns of the aspirational working families and, as a result, of allowing the Coalition to occupy the "middle ground where politics must always be contested in our nation." The *Australian* expressed real contempt for the social types now leading Labor. On three occasions it repeated a comment of Kim Beazley Sr: "When I joined the Labor Party, it contained the cream of the working class. But as I look about me now, all I see are the dregs of the middle class." One of the canonical pieces for the *Australian* on the question of the folly of Labor's embrace of the Greens was written by Michael Costa. "Labor will never be able to match the Greens in a rhetorical battle on so-called social justice …

The Greens need to be confronted rather than appeased." Another canonical piece was written by Paul Kelly, who in deploying and distorting an argument first put by Mark Latham, divided Australia into the "insiders" – represented by the Greens and Labor – and the "outsiders" – represented by the Coalition. According to this argument, school teachers were "insiders" and mining executives "outsiders." If Labor was to prosper, it had to fight the Greens and reconnect with the values of the contemporary "working class," which turned out to be the values of the "aspirational" members of the new Australian middle class also known as "working families." According to this *Alice in Wonderland* analysis, joining a trade union was anti-working class. Kevin Rudd had been pilloried remorselessly as a social democrat. But now, following the formation of the Labor–Greens alliance, the *Australian* issued a stern warning: "The party must stand up for social democratic principles." Standing up for social democratic principles was code for attacking the Greens. In her April 2011 Whitlam Oration, Julia Gillard finally took the *Australian's* advice. "[T]he Greens will never embrace Labor's delight at sharing the values of everyday Australians, in our cities, suburbs, towns and bush. Those Australians who, day after day, do the right thing, leading purposeful and dignified lives, driven by love of family and country." The *Australian* cheered. In expressing his displeasure at these "obnoxious" remarks, Bob Brown nonetheless let it be known that they would not influence the continuation of his party's support of the Gillard government. Paul Kelly was reduced to sarcastic mockery: "How noble and honourable are these Greens."

According to the *Australian*, the Greens not only represented a contemptible section of the population – those who lived in the inner city and had a university education – but were also not really a political party at all. Time and time again the main political journalists at the *Australian* argued that the Greens simply did not understand that engagement in adult politics involved the willingness to negotiate and to compromise. On 2 December 2010, the *Australian* argued: "It's time for the Greens to decide whether they are in parliament to put their stamp on legislation or stamp their feet." On 29 January 2011, it advised: "If the Greens want policy change they should act like a mature political party not a permanent protest movement." Nor could there be any doubt about what issue would provide the critical test for the Greens on this point. The issue would be the carbon price. Paul Kelly put it like this as early as November 2010. "The Greens have a choice. They can stay at the table and join the compromises that deliver a carbon price or they can knife Gillard the way they knifed Rudd." The same point was made even more emphatically in an editorial seven months later. Unless the Greens were able to agree to compromises over the design of the carbon tax, they would go down in history as "climate vandals."

On 10 July the Gillard government announced the details of its carbon tax. The Greens had won clear concessions, most importantly a $10 billion renewable-energy investment fund. But regarding everything else – most importantly, the price of carbon and the compensation packages for both businesses and citizens – they had got very much less than they had wanted. In the history of the evolution of the Greens as a political party, the capacity they had shown to compromise, even on matters of the greatest possible significance to them, represented a true turning point.

In the days following the announcement the Greens were roundly attacked by the *Australian* on standard neoliberal grounds. "The Gillard government has been accused of distorting the clean energy fund to favour the Greens' pet projects ..." "The flaws in the Gillard government's broadly rational carbon tax package have a common stain: the mark of Green fingerprints." The Greens had supposedly "compromised" the market-based principles of the plan. Not once were they praised for having shown the capacity to compromise. This was not merely churlish. Because of the single-mindedness of the war of propaganda that it was waging against the Greens, the *Australian* was blind to the historical significance of this moment.

In September 2010, if not before, Bob Brown had taken the decision to oppose this propaganda war. In his back-page column in the summer edition of *Green* magazine, Brown pointed out that one of the journalists at the *Australian*, Ean Higgins, had written inquiring whether he was running a campaign against the paper. "No, just standing up to you, Ean, I replied. Now there is a much wider public debate about *The Australian*'s censorious, biased, unethical, pro-plutocracy, anti-democracy, self-serving impact on the nation's affairs." And in early April, in pointing to the fact that the NSW branch of the party had gone against his advice with regard to the Israel question in the recent state election, Brown remarked: "*The Australian* will drive it for all it is worth because they have an anti-Greens agenda. But the hate media doesn't set our policy, we set it." It was, however, on 19 May 2011, at a Canberra press gallery conference, that with seeming spontaneity Brown finally put his whole case.

James Massola had asked a question about fabrication and shysterism. Brown told him that the story he had just written about Brown's attitude to the actions of the Wilderness Society was a good example. "I think we've got to look at fabrication and shysterism all over the place." Massola asked him to stop "sledging" the *Australian* and get back to the issue of asylum seekers. Brown continued:

> Yes, I'm being on the front foot for the reason that the media, with some very good exceptions, can at times lose track of the fact that it's part of the process of moving Australia into a much more secure future … I'm just not wanting to see the heat put on this country and its future. Some heat needs to go back onto those sections of the media which are trying to drag this process down … You look at the front page of some of the papers today and the commentary on this process, and it's not balanced. It is opinionated. It's not news in terms of having both sides of a story. It's not what you would read in countries around the world and I think that needs taking on. Yes, *The Australian* … I think the Murdoch media is doing a great disservice to this nation in perhaps the most important debate of the century so far.

By now it was not only Brown who was concerned about the malign influence of both the *Australian* and the Murdoch press more generally. The concern was felt inside the Gillard cabinet. In late April 2011 Chris Mitchell's close friend and deputy, Paul Whittaker, the editor of the *Australian*, was appointed by News Limited as editor-in-chief of the Sydney tabloid the *Daily Telegraph*. Senior members of the cabinet believed that Whittaker had been instructed by the head of News Limited in Australia, John Hartigan, to inject into the *Daily Telegraph* the aggressive style and tone that had become the trademark of the *Australian*. In particular, they believed that Hartigan had given Whittaker riding instructions to duplicate those remorseless anti-government campaigns – concerning home insulation, the Building the Education Revolution program and, more recently, the National Broadband Network – that had once so successfully undermined the Rudd government and that were now undermining its successor. What the cabinet most dreaded was that the *Daily Telegraph* would begin to campaign against the carbon tax – something which, following the appointment of Whittaker, it surely did.

There was another profound anxiety that was felt by certain members of the Gillard government. In late April or early May, Rupert Murdoch had invited some of his Australian editors and leading journalists for a meeting at Carmel in California. In our interview Chris Mitchell told me he had been at this meeting and that on the second day Australia's domestic political situation had been discussed. Leaks from the meeting had reached some members of Cabinet. At the meeting, it was learned, there had been discussion about how the Australian national interest was being compromised by a minority government which relied for the success of its stability and its legislative program on the party that Rupert Murdoch had recently described as "the bloody Greens." News Limited controlled 70 per cent of Australia's national and statewide press. Tony Abbott had staked his leadership on a campaign to destroy the carbon tax that the Gillard government was determined to introduce. Introducing a carbon tax in the absence of bipartisanship was fraught with political danger. If the leading editors and journalists of the Murdoch press had indeed been encouraged at Carmel to throw their newspapers' weight behind an anti-carbon tax campaign, it was almost inevitable that the Gillard government would not merely be defeated but destroyed at the next election. On the other hand, members of the government understood that there was hardly a more risky strategy in Australian politics than to take an open stand against the Murdoch press. There was great uncertainty about what ought now to be done.

In early July, two events intersected. In the United Kingdom the illegal phone-hacking affair erupted. As discussed earlier, resignations and arrests of some of News International's most senior executives followed shortly. In Australia, simultaneously, the Gillard government released the details of its plans for the carbon tax, which would almost certainly determine the government's fate. Public-opinion polls showed the Labor Party with a primary vote between 26 and 28 per cent. This was lower than at any time in its history. As the Murdoch empire had been so suddenly and dramatically weakened, government ministers spoke out. The most important critic of News Limited and the *Australian*, Senator Stephen Conroy, now talked openly about his belief that the Murdoch press was intent on "regime change" and about what he believed had happened at Carmel. He was particularly concerned about the astonishing bias revealed on a daily basis by Paul Whittaker's *Daily Telegraph*. So, we now learned, was the treasurer, Wayne Swan. Even the cautious prime minister, Julia Gillard, thought that events in Britain raised questions about News Limited that needed to be answered.

For years the ABC and the Fairfax press had failed to discuss with the seriousness it demanded the problem that the Murdoch press posed for the health of Australian democracy. They had not even answered the *Australian*'s never-ending insults about their incompetence and left-wing bias. Now at last there was a sign of change. An editorial in the *Sunday Age* on 17 July went to the heart of the matter:

> [H]acking isn't the story in Australia … The real issue with News
> Limited is its dominance of the print media. Murdoch owns 70 per

cent of Australian newspapers, compared with 40 per cent in Britain. That in itself is unhealthy in our view, but it becomes more of a problem if News, as its accusers charge, has a culture of routinely distorting the news for its own commercial purposes, bullies people who dare to criticise it, and is so biased on contentious issues such as climate change that it corrupts public debate … Britain's Deputy Prime Minister, Nick Clegg, says the atmosphere is now "a little like an end to the dictatorship when everyone suddenly discovers they were against the dictator." *Telegraph* columnist, Charles Moore, wrote that the Prime Minister David Cameron's admission that politicians "had turned a blind eye" to media wrongs because they were desperate for electoral endorsement has "broken the spell" of Rupert Murdoch … [W]ith few exceptions the "British spring" when it comes to Rupert Murdoch has not yet been exported to Australia. Most politicians are loath to speak publicly against powerful media operators. If ever there was a moment to do so, this is it.

On the ABC's 7.30 Chris Uhlmann, a journalist who had recently been praised by Janet Albrechtsen for his interrogation of Bob Brown, outlined with precision the anger about News Limited's behaviour felt by cabinet ministers, by Bob Brown and by one of the independents supporting the government, Rob Oakeshott. Viewers were reminded of Brown's description of the *Australian* as the "hate media." They learned that Oakeshott regarded News Limited's treatment of him as "malicious." Uhlmann's report was followed by a Leigh Sales interview with the head of News Limited, John Hartigan. Hartigan answered the question about hacking in Australia convincingly. In his experience the British tabloids were in a class of their own. More interesting, however, were three probably inadvertent admissions. Hartigan conceded that "We've been very aggressive with Rob Oakeshott." He characterised the political reporting of the *Australian* as "strident." He even let slip what had been leaked about the political discussions at Carmel. "[W]e have things that we think as a company and individually as editors that need to be done. One of them is a leadership vacuum by minority government ..." Extraordinarily enough, what Hartigan was saying here was that what the "company" that owned 70 per cent of the Australian press wanted "done" was to bring to an end the "leadership vacuum" that had been created by the formation of the minority Gillard government. In the political context, this was an admission that News Limited was indeed actively working to bring about "regime change."

The collapse of the reputation of the British arm of the Murdoch empire led to a rather muddled debate about its implications for Australia. According to one line of thought, articulated by Paul Keating – the politician who had been responsible for giving Rupert Murdoch 70 per cent of the Australian press in 1987 – the issue raised did not go beyond the legal protection of privacy. According to another, raised by the federal secretary of the Media Entertainment and Arts Alliance, Chris Warren, in a letter to the prime minister, the fundamental issue was diversity of opinion and the Murdoch stranglehold over the ownership of Australian newspapers. And according to yet another, put most vividly by Stephen Conroy, the central issue was the systemic anti-Labor bias of the Murdoch press and its determination to engineer regime change. According, however, to Bob Brown, the overwhelming question was not privacy nor ownership nor bias. It was all three. The question of privacy and ownership and bias demanded a thoroughgoing parliamentary investigation.

Readers of this essay will not be surprised by the attitude taken to these questions at the *Australian*. Sadly, it argued, Mr Murdoch had been betrayed by those who worked for *News of the World*. As a busy man who employed 53,000 people across the globe, he could not be expected to know what was happening in each individual newspaper. If Murdoch had chosen any other business, he would have been treated as a hero. He was now the victim of a "feeding frenzy." Why? In part it was because he was still regarded as a threat to the conservative British establishment whom he had discomfited when he took over the *Times*. In addition, his "varied, vibrant and influential media entities" were a "focus of resentment, if not hate" among the "progressive establishment" in the "bureaucracies, public broadcasters and universities" of the English-speaking world. In the face of all this undeserved hostility, the *Australian* thought Rupert Murdoch now had reason to ask himself the question posed by Franz Kafka in *The Trial*: "What is the charge?" The *Australian* was appalled at the "creeping opportunism" shown by the Gillard government in trying to take advantage of the problems Murdoch faced because of the behaviour of the few bad apples at *News of the World*. Any suggestion that there were any problems with the Murdoch press in Australia were "repugnant." Particularly repugnant were the statements of Senator Conroy, who at other times had tried to "ingratiate" himself at the *Australian*. "It is a sorry time in national affairs when a struggling minister can use compliant arms of the media to launch facile tirades at the only media prepared to hold the government to account." Claims about a desire at the *Australian* for "regime change" were both "insulting and desperate." So were the predictable attempts of its incompetent Fairfax commercial rivals and the publicly funded ABC to use the problems of News International in Britain to "settle old scores." Nor was the *Australian* in the least surprised by the antics of Bob Brown. He was partial to the publicly funded media because he thought that "the profit motive corrupts." He had made no secret of his "disdain" for the *Australian*. His disdain was founded on the fact that the *Australian* was the only newspaper to hold his party to account. The *Australian* would fight his "troubling" desire for press regulation. "We will not be intimidated into giving Senator Brown, or anyone else, an easy ride."

Rupert Murdoch described himself on the day he appeared before the House of Commons as humbled. Humility was not the mood of his most influential Australian lieutenant. As the only true defender of journalistic rigour and integrity in Australia, Chris Mitchell imagined himself surrounded by a vicious gang of media incompetents and political failures. He would not submit to their bullying.

AUSTRALIA'S MURDOCH PROBLEMS

Australia has not one Murdoch problem but two. The first is the more straightforward. The fact that News Limited owns 70 per cent of the newspapers in Australia represents a threat to the flourishing of an open democratic culture. If Rupert Murdoch, the chairman and chief executive of News Corporation, was an apolitical or a distant figure, the threat might be merely notional. He is, however, not only a highly political individual with a powerful set of ideological beliefs. He is also determined to maintain tight control over the political line of all his papers on issues that interest him, as he did before the invasion of Iraq. In addition, he appears to have an almost paternal concern for what he sees as the wellbeing of Australia.

For these reasons, I can think of no plausible argument that could justify his company's control of 70 per cent of Australia's newspaper market. The issue is not the absence of alternative sources of information for politically engaged citizens. In the age of the internet there are hundreds of easily accessible sources of information. The issue is rather the capacity of News Limited to influence the opinions of the vast majority of less engaged citizens whose political understanding is shaped directly by the popular newspapers and indirectly through the commercial radio and television programs which rely on the daily papers for the content of their programs and, more deeply, for the way they interpret the world. As already argued, evidence suggests that at the meeting of News Limited editors and key journalists at Carmel earlier this year, discussion took place about the need to do something about the minority Gillard government and its untenable alliance with the far left-wing Greens. Following that meeting, the key Murdoch tabloids began to campaign in earnest against the government and in particular against its carbon tax. This example demonstrates that News Limited's control of 70 per cent of Australia's newspaper market is no longer a merely potential problem. It poses a real and present danger to the health of Australian democracy.

The Murdoch stranglehold over the daily press must be challenged and broken. The current weakening of Murdoch's grip on his global empire at a time when the Gillard government controls the House of Representatives and the Greens hold the balance of power in the Senate presents a unique window of opportunity. The question, of course, is whether the government is willing to take what would undoubtedly be an extraordinary and perhaps unacceptable risk.

The second problem Murdoch poses for this country is the *Australian*. Under Chris Mitchell's editorship, as I have tried to show, the *Australian* has played the role not so much of reporter or interpreter but rather of national enforcer of those values that lie at the heart of the Murdoch empire: market fundamentalism and the beneficence of American global hegemony. Unquestioning support for American foreign policy led it to the conduct of an extraordinarily strident campaign in favour of an invasion that was launched on the basis of false intelligence, that has been responsible for perhaps 400,000 deaths, and for which it has never uttered a word of apology. The *Australian* has conducted a prolonged and intellectually incoherent campaign against action on climate change, which has undermined the hold in public life of the central values of the Enlightenment, Science and Reason. This has helped make action by any Australian government on the most serious question of contemporary times far more difficult than it ought to have been. It has conducted a series of high-volume and unbalanced campaigns directed against Labor governments, in which its journalists, rather than investigating a problem with an open mind, have often sought out evidence in support of a pre-determined editorial conclusion. The *Australian* has consistently attempted to turn ideas with which it disagrees, especially those that its editor-in-chief associates with that hydra-headed monster known as the Left, into un-Australian heresies. It has sought systematically to undermine the credibility of its only broadsheet rivals – the *Sydney Morning Herald* and the *Age* – and, in a relentless campaign, to intimidate and drive towards the Right the only other mainstream source of analysis and opinion in this country, the ABC.

The *Australian* has pursued its many, often radically unequal enemies, mercilessly and sometimes unscrupulously. It has conducted a kind of jihad against one party, the Greens, that has the support of one and a half million of the nation's citizens. By its own admission it has devoted itself to the task of trying to have that party destroyed at the ballot box, a statement which in itself undermines any claim to fairness or to balance. And perhaps most importantly of all, in the guise of a traditional broadsheet newspaper, the *Australian* has turned itself into a player in national politics without there being any means by which its actions can be held to account. It claims that it is held accountable by commercial reality. According to those who understand such matters, its financial situation is altogether opaque. Ironically, even though its core value is the magic of the market, it is very doubtful if it could have survived in the past or could survive in the present without hidden financial subsidy from the global empire of its founding father, Rupert Murdoch, for whom the *Australian* has offered the most important means for influencing politics and commerce in the country of his birth.

It is reasonably easy, at least in theory, to suggest a solution to the problem posed by the Murdoch empire's ownership of 70 per cent of the Australian press. It is not at all easy to find a solution to the problem of the *Australian*. Even though there are good grounds for strengthening the legal protection of privacy, there is almost nothing to suggest that this would influence its behaviour. I know of no evidence that the *Australian* or indeed any News Limited paper has engaged in phone hacking or any equivalent practices of the kind that have corrupted the practice of journalism in the United Kingdom. In Australia, newspapers are regulated by the laws against defamation and racial hatred and the complaints processes available to citizens and corporations through action before the Press Council. I cannot imagine and most likely would not support any additional legal or quasi-legal means for the monitoring or the punishment of press bias.

With regard to the problem of the *Australian*, I can think only of one possible solution: courageous external and internal criticism. During the conduct of research for this essay, several people have discussed the strange passivity of the two mainstream rivals of the *Australian*, the Fairfax press and the ABC, even in the face of a constant barrage of criticism and lampooning. This is not only a mistake with regard to the self-interest of both organisations; it has also left the victims of the *Australian*'s attacks vulnerable and friendless. There is an old joke that suggests that no individual ought to engage in battle with those who buy their ink by the barrel. The joke does not apply to organisations which have the same arsenal of weapons at their disposal as the *Australian*. During the recent times of trouble for the Murdoch empire there have been signs of change at Fairfax and the ABC, where tough questions about the behaviour of the *Australian* and other News Limited papers have at long last been posed.

There is another dimension to the problem. In the course of my research I have become aware of considerable unease among present and former journalists at the *Australian* concerning both the political extremism and frequent irrationalism of the paper for which they work and the bullying behaviour of their editor-in-chief. If such people acted together to make their opinions known, it is not impossible that change might come. The *Australian* employs many of the best journalists in the country. I will not name them for fear of doing them harm. It only requires a different editor-in-chief and owner for it to become a truly outstanding newspaper.

15 August 2011

To continue the conversation, visit **www.robertmanne.com.au**

NOTES

The essay is based mainly on articles published by the *Australian* but also on many interviews, for the most part "off the record." On 15 June I interviewed Chris Mitchell, Paul
Kelly, Clive Mathieson, Nick Cater, Michael Stutchbury, Dennis Shanahan and Matthew
Franklin at the office of the *Australian*. It is important to point out that the case studies chosen involve what I call ideologically sensitive questions. Many aspects of the paper are not
analysed.

To avoid misunderstanding or the charge of evasion, a brief account of my relations
with Chris Mitchell and the *Australian* seems necessary. In August 1996 Mitchell devoted
seven pages of the paper he then edited, the *Courier Mail*, to something he regarded as one
of the greatest scoops in Australian history. Mitchell believed that Manning Clark, Australia's most famous historian, had received an Order of Lenin. He thought he was a high-
level Soviet spy or agent. The story collapsed in a matter of days. At the time I edited the
anti-communist magazine *Quadrant*. Mitchell tried unsuccessfully to enlist my support.
Our next encounter occurred in 2001, after I published "In Denial," a *Quarterly Essay* which
analysed the right-wing campaign against the idea of the injustice done to the stolen generations. Mitchell commissioned his then wife, Deborah Cassrels, to write an attack which
came to 7700 words. After it was published, to my considerable surprise, Mitchell urged
me to travel to Cape York at News Limited's expense to see the conditions in the Aboriginal communities there for myself, an offer I gratefully accepted. In mid-2002 Chris
Mitchell became editor-in-chief of the *Australian*. The paper became now an unwanted
presence in my life, scarcely a month passing where I was not attacked in reports, editorials, feature articles, columns, letters to the editor or the daily compendium of spleen and
schadenfreude known as "Cut and Paste." In February 2009, once again to my surprise, a
kind of truce was offered with a proposal that I contribute to the paper. Since that time I
have been treated courteously, especially by the editor of the *Weekend Australian*, Nick Cater.
Old hostilities more or less ceased.

2   "the 70 per cent of the national and statewide press he owns ...": News Limited, the
    Australian subsidiary of Murdoch's News Corporation, has interests in more than
    100 Australian newspapers. According to the Commonwealth Parliamentary
    Library, its share of circulation is 68 per cent of the capital city and national news-
    paper market, 77 per cent of the Sunday newspaper market, 62 per cent of the sub-
    urban newspaper market and 18 per cent of the regional newspaper market: Kim
    Jackson, "Media Ownership Regulation in Australia," 30 May 2006, http://www.
    aph.gov.au/library/intguide/sp/media_regulations.htm#Introduction.

4   "In no other newspaper is the spirit of the editor so omnipresent ...": In our inter-
    view, the present editor, Clive Mathieson, claimed that "Chris sets the editorial
    direction of the paper" and that "he does the big editorial philosophy of what the

paper is." He also argued that if one wanted to understand the *Australian*, "you should read the editorials ..." The editorials, he went on, were the place where "we correct the perceptions about where the paper stands on various issues. So that is pure, unplugged Chris from time to time." He argued that the paper "needs to be noisy" and that despite its small circulation it was their intention to ensure that "if you're involved in federal politics, you must read it." Interview with Clive Mathieson, 15 June 2011.

4   "the *Australian* now dominates the Canberra press gallery ...": According to Bob Brown, there are always "three or four" journalists from the *Australian* at press conferences in Canberra. "Sometimes" they constitute "more than half" of those attending. "They plan, come to a press conference saying you ask about this issue and you ask about that. It is a planned effort to try to get a drop on the victim ... It debases the profession and it cheats the public." Interview with Senator Bob Brown, 10 June 2011.

6   "Australia was founded on the basis of the destruction ...": W.E.H. Stanner, *After the Dreaming*, Australian Broadcasting Commission, Sydney 1969; C.D. Rowley, *The Destruction of Aboriginal Society; The Remote Aborigines; Outcasts in White Society*, Penguin, Ringwood, 1972 (first published 1970): Henry Reynolds, *Aborigines and Settlers*, Cassell, North Melbourne, 1972; *The Other Side of the Frontier*, History Department, James Cook University, 1981.

6   "In late 2002 Keith Windschuttle published ...": Keith Windschuttle, *The Fabrication of Aboriginal History: Volume One, Van Diemen's Land*, Macleay Press, Sydney, 2002.

6   "Lemkin himself wrote extensively on the question of the destruction ...": Ann Curthoys, "Raphael Lemkin on Tasmania" in A. Dirk Moses and Dan Stone (eds.), *Colonialism and Genocide*, Routledge, New York and London, 2007. Lyndall Ryan, *The Aboriginal Tasmanians*, University of Queensland Press, St Lucia, 1981; Henry Reynolds, *An Indelible Stain?: The Question of Genocide in Australia's History*, Penguin, Ringwood, 2001.

8   "Compare words taken from the concluding passage ...": John West, *The History of Tasmania* (edited by A.G.L. Shaw), Angus and Robertson, Sydney, 1971 (first published 1852). The words quoted are found on pp. 310 and 333.

10   "a critical anthology I had edited ...": Robert Manne (ed.), *Whitewash: On Keith Windschuttle's Fabrication of Aboriginal History*, Black Inc., Melbourne, 2003.

11   "Windschuttle published two further books ...": Keith Windschuttle, *The White Australia Policy*, Macleay Press, Sydney, 2004; Keith Windschuttle, *The Fabrication of Aboriginal History: The Stolen Generations*, Macleay Press, Sydney, 2010.

13   "Aborigines have had a hard time of it ...": Gary Johns, *Aboriginal Self-Determination: The White Man's Dream*, Connor Court, Ballan, 2011, pp. 301–2.

13–14 "balanced against those of Pearson ... Pearson understands the dire implication ...": Noel Pearson, *Up From the Mission: Selected Writings*, Black Inc., Melbourne, 2009, p. 350.

15   "The argument of the war party ...": For the official argument, see *The National Security*

Strategy of the United States of America, White House, Washington, September 2002.

16   "Rupert Murdoch was so close to the war ...": Jamie Doward et al., "Phone-hacking scandal: is this the tipping point for Murdoch's empire?," guardian.co.uk, July 9 2011. Roy Greenslade, "Their master's voice," *The Guardian*, February 17, 2003.

20–21 "as Blix argued in his memoir ...": Hans Blix, *Disarming Iraq*, Pantheon Books, New York, 2004, pp.138–43.

22   This breezy editorial was in part penned ...": In an email of 16 June 2011, Salusinszky confirmed that he had input into the editorial of 12 April 2003, "Coaltion of the whining got it wrong."

22   "most plausible figure for civilian deaths ... between 300,000 and 400,000 ...": I have arrived at this figure in the following way. According to the Iraq Body Count there have been 106,000 recorded deaths attributable to the consequences of the invasion and occupation of Iraq. This figure is based on media reports and reports of the Iraqi government and NGOs. In an interview with BBC Radio a head of Iraq Body Count thought that the real death toll since the invasion was between two and three times higher, that is between 200,000 and 300,000. A survey of post-invasion Iraq conducted by Johns Hopkins University in the United States and published in *The Lancet* estimated some 650,000 "excess deaths." An official from the British Ministry of Defence regarded its methodology as "robust." Opinion Research Business estimated excess deaths at over one million, but its methodology is widely regarded as unreliable. Between 300,000 and 400,000 represents the mid-point between the lowest possible and the highest plausible estimate. An excellent brief discussion can be found in "Counting bodies: how many people were killed in the Iraq war?" *BBC World Service*, 27 August 2010.

24   "Sheridan is a man who argued in different columns ...": For these Sheridan comments, *The Australian*, 27 January 2003, 17 July 2008, 5 and 11 September 2008, 7 February 2009, 27 March 2010.

27   "Koestler coined a very useful neologism ...": Arthur Koestler (ed.), *Suicide of a Nation?*, Macmillan, New York, 1964.

37   "As you consider climate change legislation ...": http://www.aass.org/news/releases/2009/media/1021climate_letter.pdf. The eighteen signatories were the American Association for the Advancement of Science, the American Chemical Society, the American Geophysical Union, the American Institute of Biological Sciences, the American Meterological Society, the American Society of Agronomy, the American Society of Plant Biologists, the American Statistical Association, the Association of Ecosystem Research Centers, the Botanical Society of America, the Crop Science Society of America, the Ecological Society of America, the Natural Science Collections Alliance, the Organization of Biological Field Stations, the Society for Industrial and Applied Mathematics, the Society of Systematic Biologists, the Soil Science Society of America and the University Corporation for Atmospheric Research.

40 "Some of the best qualified ...": James Hansen, *Storms of My Grandchildren*, Bloomsbury, New York, 2009, p. 250.

42 "The entry into the debate ...": Ian Plimer, *Heaven and Earth: Global Warming, The Missing Science*, Connor Court, Ballan, 2009.

50 "By the use of a Factiva newspaper database formula ...": The formula used was **ns=gclimt and se=features**

56 "In March 2006 the prime minister launched ...": ABC Radio National, *The Media Report*, 9 March 2006.

62 "Bush had been working on G20 matters ...": Lenore Taylor and David Uren, *Shitstorm: Inside Labor's Darkest Days*, Melbourne University Press, Carlton, 2010, pp. 128–9.

63 "Rudd's authorship of a long essay ...": Kevin Rudd, "The Global Financial Crisis," *The Monthly*, February 2009.

70–71 "Far more problematic, however ...": *Building the Education Revolution. Implementation Taskforce: Final Report*, 8 July 2011. The following passage is from the media release. "This unique program has delivered economic stimulus and major new investment in school infrastructure that in the vast majority of cases is much appreciated by school principals and their communities and which will improve educational outcomes for years ahead. BER has however been the subject of valid complaints from approximately 3% of school communities."

73 "the announcement of a super profits tax on mining proceeds ...": The mining super profits tax was introduced at a time when the price of many minerals, and therefore mining profits, had reached historically high levels. There were two main purposes of the tax. The first was to help fund a rise in the rate of superannuation from 9 to 12 per cent. The second was to lower company tax so as to help those sectors of the economy – especially manufacturing and tourism – badly affected by the commodity price–driven rise in the value of the Australian dollar, a problem known to economists as "the Dutch disease."

79 "In response to the Massola article ...": Greg Jericho, "Spartacus No More," *Grog's Gamut*, 27 September 2010.

80 "Posetti hit back on the *Drum* ...": Julie Posetti, "The Australian. Think. Again." *The Drum*, 5 October 2010.

81 "Asa Wahlquist spoke briefly on a panel at the conference ...": The recording of Asa Wahlquist's talk is at "Tape of the Tweet," *Crikey*, 30 November 2010.

84 "Milan Kundera's first novel ...": Milan Kundera, *The Joke*, Coward-McCann, New York, 1969.

94 "Isaiah Berlin once argued ...": Isaiah Berlin, "The Hedgehog and the Fox: An Essay on Tolstoy's View of History" in Isaiah Berlin (author), Henry Hardy and Aileen Kelly (eds), *Russian Thinkers*, Viking Press, New York, 1978.

106 "Brown finally put his whole case ...": http://bob-brown.greensmps.org.au/content/greencast/bob-brown-press-conference-may-19-2011.

FAIR SHARE	*Correspondence*

John van Tiggelen

It's always a pleasant surprise to see a southerner take Bob Katter seriously. He's no fool to act like one in a place that suffers them gladly. But the man does bleat. Waddawe want? A fair share! When do we want it? Now! When did we ever not? Ah, anyone seen my hat?

Judith Brett has written a succinct history of country–city relations. But try as I might, I could not make out an argument for a new national compact between the three. Or is it four? Whatever; metropolitan and regional and rural and remote and Aboriginal Australia do not make two, any more than the former Country, now National Party, ever represented Wollongong or Palm Island.

The essay pivots on the contention that "the agents of neoliberalism cut the country loose from the city and left it to fend for itself." Consequently, country Australia has been in a state of crisis for a generation. And sure, bits of it are. Necessary reforms such as the abolition of tariffs, deregulation and the amalgamation of one-town shires meant there were losers. So did less neces-sary developments, such as the emergence of a supermarket duopoly and the spectacular rise and fall of managed investment schemes. But there were windfalls and winners, too; and besides, not all change can be sheeted home to neoliberalism: opportunities in the mines, for instance, sucked thousands of workers from the land.

The question is, has the fabric of country life been weakened more in the last generation than in those previous? In generations past, rural Australia's eco-nomic contribution, augmented by protectionism, jingoism and Menzies-style paternalism, helped elevate the country's standing in both its own eyes and those of city folk. But parts were always in crisis. The advent of motorised transport, the closure of railways, world war sacrifice, rabbit plagues, ten-year droughts, the collapse of soldier settlements, mass plantings of pine trees, the decommissioning of mines and the ever-broadening economies of scale broke the back of hundreds of country communities. Really, were the good old days that much better? Why should last year's closure of the cheese factory in Leitchville, northern Victoria, matter any more, in a nation-building context, than the closure of the butter factory in my home town of Dumbalk, South Gippsland, in the early '70s?

Butter factories have been closing for a hundred years. So have sawmills, schools, butchers, bakeries, hospitals, railway lines, river ports and abattoirs. These contractions are easy to miss, because so much of the nation's settlement has been too fleeting to leave ruins. Hundreds of racecourses, back then a horse-and-buggy ride apart, have vanished without trace thoughout south-eastern Australia. It's like there's a second Dreaming, layered on the original: are the ghostly campfires ringing Lake Buloke, in the Wimmera, those of Aboriginal tribes gathering on its shores to catch eels? Or are they those of the 10,000-plus men that massed here every autumn from the 1870s to the 1970s for the opening of duck-shooting season?

Swathes of the land are emptying: every lone church represented a community once. At the same time parts are replenishing: those churches are now the renovation dreams of tree-changers.

Out west and up north, the landscape's never been rural. Brett twice quotes the following lines from Katter: "I mean, if you drop a series of hydrogen bombs from the back of Cairns, the other side of Mareeba … all the way across to Broome, you won't kill anybody. There's nobody living there."

Well, yes, we've pretty much left the tropical savannah to termites, feral pigs and hump-shouldered beasts bound for Indonesia. Katter asserts 60 million people could comfortably live there, like he does, but it's not as if people haven't tried. The first town "the other side of Mareeba" is Dimbulah, a once-humming centre of the Far North's tobacco industry. Tobacco farming was an early (and reasonable) casualty of globalisation, and in the two decades since, Dimbulah has been in the throes of various government-sponsored "quit" programs – tea-tree plantations, outback tourism and annual wheelbarrow races. The results aren't pretty.

Doubtless Katter has towns like Dimbulah in mind when he laments, as quoted by Brett: "I've watched towns literally close down before my eyes." Of course, he's exaggerating: dying towns don't close down. They just become more dysfunctional. The North's interior is dotted with the *Wake in Fright*–style leftovers of the fettler and drover communities that once beaded a vast, dendritic network of railway tracks channelling ore and cattle to the coast. Take, for instance, the remaining line heading west through Katter's home town of Charters Towers to his birthplace of Cloncurry. The whistle-stops along this 600-kilometre strip constitute the full spectrum of extinction. Hughenden and Richmond compete for tourists with rival fossil festivals and dinosaur museums. Balfes Creek, Homestead, Pentland, Torrens Creek and Prairie cling desperately to their eponymous hotels. Pub-less Maxwelton and Nelia are ghost towns – last time I was in "Maxy" you could buy a home for $5000. And Thalanga, Boree, Oombabia, Mumu and Nonda struggle to be remembered at all, having vanished well before neoliberalism began levelling playing fields.

Meanwhile, elsewhere in Katter country, towns thrive. His vast electorate includes the desert mining centre of Mount Isa as well as the sugar-cane coast between Cairns and Townsville, sustained by the nation's wettest catchments. Innisfail, re-roofed after Cyclone Larry, has never looked shinier. Tully is undergoing a similar makeover, post-Yasi. And the tourism future of beautiful Mission Beach appears assured, with or without the endangered cassowary, and with or without the imperilled reef, for that matter.

So what might a city–country compact achieve in Katterland (Kattertonia)? For all of Katter's yammering, it's not as though his voters have been forsaken. During my ten years in the North, I lost count of the number of government rescue and exit packages cobbled together for tobacco, dairy, sugar and banana farmers. Southern money renovated the foreshores of Cairns and Townsville, rebuilt cyclone-struck communities, subsidised mining infrastructure and infused indigenous communities to the point of abject dependency.

Brett suggests that country people no longer believe themselves "to be the true face of Australia … carrying the nation on their sturdy backs." I'm not sure about that. When I was in Townsville, the literary critic Peter Pierce, having just taken up a local academic post, observed that North Queenslanders at times affected a "cultural strut," which he defined as "the arrogant, aggressive, unreflective, self-promotion of Australianness." He hastened to add this affliction wasn't restricted to the tropics, but the description still applies, not least to Katter himself.

North Queenslanders, if local surveys are to be believed, continue to yearn for separate statehood. Indeed, local politicians do well to support the "movement," as Katter does, by feeding the misperception that North Queenslanders are being "robbed" – that is, that their resources are propping up the rest of the state, and indeed the rest of the nation. Brett briefly notes that the North's push for separation arose in the late nineteenth century out of anti-Brisbane feeling. But it was actually uglier than that. The real impetus for separation was the intention of southern colonial powers to end the North's exploitation of indentured islanders from the South Pacific, a practice known as blackbirding.

The separatist campaign to retain coolie labour was eventually overrun by the campaign for federation, but there was a recent echo of the North's dubious moral position, again posing as an economic one, in its protest against Canberra's suspension of the live cattle trade.

Brett points out that federation established the conditions for "a trade-off between the country and the city," whereby country people would receive a fair share of resources as compensation for the costs of living remotely. She argues that governments stuck to this trade-off until dismantling it in the neoliberal 1980s and 1990s, thus allowing cities to prosper at the expense of opportunities and services in the country. Now a new compact is needed to prevent country people ending up second-class citizens.

Maybe she's right. There is undue suffering, here and there. Too many farmers are committing suicide. But it remains a big call to suggest that regional, rural and remote Australians are worse off now, relative to their city cousins, than they were a generation ago.

I've lived most of my life in country Australia, and still do. I'm aware there's a country–city divide, but it has a cultural lining. There are bigger, more sinister divides to worry about, like the gaping inequality of maintaining private health and education systems for the rich.

Compact or no compact, the city will continue to need the country. On the surface, there's nothing wrong with calls to stand by our country mates. To give them a "fair go." Or something. But there's an undertow in Katter's crying poor – and Brett tugs at it too – that doing more for the bush is not just the decent, nation-building thing to do, which is all well and good, but that it's the true-blue thing to do, which gives me the heebie-jeebies.

And there's something else. Katter, like the vast majority of country people, thinks climate change science is bunkum. It's understandable: to believe in a drier future is to question your place on the land. That's a terribly unsettling thing. But denial's hardly a basis for any new compact. The last thing the people of the Murray-Darling Basin need right now is another excuse to bung their collective head in the dirt.

John van Tiggelen

Eric Knight

In 2006 I visited an indigenous town called Utopia on the edge of the Tanami Desert, in the Northern Territory. As I looked out on what stretched as far as the eye could see, I began to realise how empty our land really is. Utopia was desperately poor. Dogs scratched around the township looking for food, and old women lay in the shade of concrete dugouts. Had Utopia once been paradise? Or was it named in the hope that one day its fortunes would change? I don't know the answer, but I did know the problem with Utopia: geography.

The Bangladeshi economist and Nobel laureate Muhammad Yunus found a way to alleviate his people's poverty by offering them microfinance. Yunus' scheme worked because Bangladeshis were poor for lack of credit. Their inability to borrow condemned them to poverty, and Yunus' intervention broke this cycle.

As I travelled across the Northern Territory, I was less sure that microfinance would work in regional Australia. Distance was the outback's tyranny, not lack of credit. It took hours to travel between these communities – Yuendumu, Ali Curung, Tennant Creek. This was cattle country, and local people were held in employment by a piece of paper binding the pastoralist to his local workers. Without the cattle trade, these places were lost. It led me to a sad conclusion: perhaps some parts of regional Australia could never be rescued.

Judith Brett's *Fair Share* forces us to confront an important reality: not all of Australia is equal. No matter how industrious we are, nature prevents some communities from being self-sustaining. The afflicted communities change over time: sometimes they are driven to the brink by drought and flood, at others by the flow of economic history. Brett's essay focuses on the latter. She returns to the great promise of federation – a nation for a continent – and inspires us to our own Manifest Destiny. Her essay reflects two deep traditions in Australian political consciousness. One is conservative – the instinct to nurture local communities and protect what we have made. The other is liberal – the desire to give these communities the skills and resources they need to live the life they value.

But at times Brett takes these two traditions and arrives at strange, almost romantic, conclusions. She advocates for subsidising the country and mounts a number of justifications for why – food security, aesthetic pleasure and nation-building. "Rural and regional Australia might always need a fair degree of subsidisation," she writes, and "we do all need to share the cost."

These are all excellent reasons for why we must do *something*. But whether the answer is simply to subsidise the country – that I am less sure of.

Judith Brett seems to suggest that the answers do not reside in a neoliberal state. It is not always clear what she means by this term. Certainly, it is hard to justify a system which lacks support for the underprivileged or a sense of decency towards our culture and history. But is that really what characterised the two and a half decades of government from 1983 onwards? Throughout the essay Brett is biting: "Neoliberalism treated farms as businesses, and farmers as business owners and entrepreneurs." Her words ring with disapproval. She argues that the promise of "adjustment" between city and country was not fulfilled. Instead of conserving the old splendour of country towns, proud families and institutions were ripped apart. Banks were replaced with ATMs, and institutions like Australia Post corporatised. It hardly sounds appealing, but it begs the question: would we be better off without ATMs?

We will always struggle to find the right balance between change and conservation. Perhaps we would be better off without ATMs because that would preserve banks as meeting places in regional towns. But at times Brett rails against "neoliberalism" when she is really talking about "economics," against change when she is describing progress.

When you look at the economic changes afoot in regional Australia, perhaps things are not as dead as Brett suggests. Mining is flourishing, yet the mining sector – the modern heart of rural Australia both economically and politically – gets only a brief hearing in the essay. It features almost as an apology, a concession to the fact that our grand vision for Australia's economic prosperity fell short. Fashioning a modern industrialised economy was the Hawke–Keating dream, but Brett is decisive in her judgment: "although it achieved a good deal, we now know that in essence it failed."

The changing political landscape of regional Australia is one of the most interesting stories in contemporary politics. Power is moving from agricultural wealth to mining wealth. Both fortunes are closely tied to geography. Agriculture depends on the soil and weather, mining on natural deposits. But the two constituencies wield power differently. Farmers are independent entrepreneurs, each one able (to some extent) to shape their economic future. Miners, by contrast, are often agglomerations of power: union and corporate. Regional towns such as Karratha and Dampier are not necessarily shaped by local residents. They are shaped by individual companies or, in the case of Andrew Forrest, by individual mining magnates. This story is missing from Brett's essay, but it is important to any understanding of what is happening in the regions.

In the mid-nineteenth century, another mining boom – the gold rush – brought immense wealth to regional Australia. Prospectors' discoveries turned quiet agricultural settlements like Ballarat and Bendigo into boom towns. The populations of these places grew, infrastructure was built, and they became prosperous, self-sustaining regional hubs.

Today's challenge is to convert the present mining boom into something similar, but the answers are often more subtle than mere subsidy. When it was recently reported that a Chinese mining company had bought agricultural land in Gunnedah, the community was outraged. It was said to be a crisis of sovereignty, with the Chinese taking control of our food and land. But foreigners have owned equity in our country for over a century. The real issue was the complex question of securing the community's long-term prosperity. Mines have a habit of expiring, and gravel pits can seldom be returned to prime agriculture. A better answer may be to encourage activity like mining on the condition that the long-term economic interests of the community are considered. Companies might be asked to invest in country Australia by building the schools, roads, rails and houses which will sustain these areas for more than a generation. Mining may not be a glamorous business, but it may be a vehicle for encouraging employment, delivering skills and building the hardware of the future economy.

At times Brett seems eager to insulate the romantic Australian bush legend from the grime of commerce. But it was commerce that first brought farming families to the land. They were enticed by the promise of profiting from the sheep's back and the fecundity of our pastures. To celebrate the economic forces which installed nineteenth-century society but regret those of modern times seems a little one-eyed. In the end, our goal is not to preserve these *places* as museum pieces of Australian history. It is to find the best way to enable these *people* to lead lives which are rich, courageous and free.

Eric Knight

Jon Altman

In *Fair Share* Judith Brett evocatively notes that Australian indigenous people for a long time occupied a space "on the edge of the nation's consciousness." She also notes that today 70 per cent live outside the cities and that Noel Pearson's goal of an economic base for such communities is crucially important. Brett then effectively eschews this section of rural Australia in her analysis. This bifurcation of black and white that subjects the two populations to separate analysis is commonplace. I want to challenge such an approach.

Two things have fundamentally altered for indigenous people in the last few decades. First, with land rights and then native title, legal recognition of indigenous ancestral lands has grown rapidly. Today, 23 per cent of the continent is either under indigenous ownership or covered by successful native-title determinations. Brett notes the dual meaning of the term "country" in English: rurality as well as nation. But in recent discourse there is a third use of the word, based on continuity of Aboriginal tradition and connection. An emerging set of new Aboriginal-English idioms deployed by indigenous people, such as "caring for country" and "working on country," takes the notion of country well beyond Brett's dualism and has even found a place in policy parlance.

Second, indigenous people have recently come to occupy a different place in the national consciousness due to the heightened awareness of deep and troubling disadvantage, especially since the Northern Territory intervention in 2007; and then, following Kevin Rudd's 2008 apology to the Stolen Generations, with the commitment to close the gap between indigenous and non-indigenous. While social indicators show that indigenous disadvantage is everywhere, most effort and money is directed at discrete communities in remote and regional Australia.

Brett ends *Fair Share* by seeking a recalibration in relations between the city and the country, with more focus given to the strengths and potential of the country. What prospects might this give indigenous communities?

The geographer John Holmes documents a transition in tropical Australia from industry and agriculture to tourism and conservation, in the form of services to preserve environmental values and biodiversity. A mapping of indigenous lands onto natural resource atlases shows that these are some of Australia's most intact areas of high conservation value. Consequently, more and more of the indigenous estate is being included in the conservation estate through the declaration of Indigenous Protected Areas. There are currently forty-two such areas, covering 230,000 square kilometres and constituting 24 per cent of Australia's National Reserve system.

While there is a dominant view that remote Aboriginal Australia is dysfunctional and unproductive, community-based ranger groups spread across the indigenous estate are delivering environmental, biosecurity, coast-watch and carbon-abatement services funded by the federal government, multinational corporations and environmental philanthropists. The dominant narrative pays little heed to such contributions.

Indigenous people are members of Norforce. John Sanderson, the retired head of the Australian Army, has noted that the population presence in northern Australia is important for national defence. And while there are some who advocate for indigenous migration off the indigenous estate for employment, if we are to continue to populate the continent it makes little sense for the recent legal rejection of *terra nullius* to be followed by a policy goal of *terra vacua* – a landscape populated by no one.

As the twenty-first century unfolds, projections indicate that the indigenous population in rural Australia will grow in both absolute and relative terms and that the indigenous estate will also grow, due to indigenous land-use agreements. At the same time, the national dependence on indigenous land for mineral extraction, conservation benefit, carbon abatement and clean energy generation will escalate. So there seems to be much economic potential and need for a future recalibration of relations.

An enduring message from *Fair Share* is that political representation in Canberra and political alliance-building are crucial to getting a fair share. One is left to ponder: how differently might development have gone if indigenous people were afforded suffrage and reserved positions in parliament after federation, as enjoyed by Maori representatives in the New Zealand parliament since the nineteenth century? And how might our political system be reconfigured so that rural indigenous Australians acquire the voice, political leverage and associated benefits enjoyed by white rural dwellers?

Jon Altman

Linda Botterill

As Judith Brett points out, the nation is quick to embrace rural iconography when we present ourselves to the world through advertising and in the opening ceremony of the Sydney 2000 Olympics (with the yellow Driza-Bones of the 1988 Seoul Olympics perhaps best forgotten). We also buy into much of the agrarian belief in the essential virtue of farming as a way of life and the "special needs" of rural folk. We are concerned about finding marriage partners for farmers, but we have not yet seen *The Plumber Wants a Wife*. Television programs such as *A Country Practice, Blue Heelers* and *McLeod's Daughters* play to our ideas of the unsophisticated, quirky rural inhabitants with hearts of gold winning over jaded and cynical city types. The television quiz show *Who Wants To Be a Millionaire?* had a special farmers edition in mid-2005 and after the last farmer departed with $32,000, the Channel Nine website reported that, "Over the past weeks, a total of $205,000 has been won by the farmers, easing some of their strain as they continue to battle the poor conditions."

However, this broad sympathy is rarely informed by the relevant policy debates, which take place among a relatively small group. While many people remember the privatisation debates concerning Qantas, the Commonwealth Bank and Telstra, few were aware of the lengthy debate over the privatisation of the Australian Wheat Board in the mid-1990s. That privatisation ended with the retention of an export monopoly in the hands of a private company, AWB Limited, with a rather peculiar share structure that privileged one group of shareholders over another. Media attention did not focus on the wheat exporter until it became embroiled in the Oil-for-Food scandal, and then reports provided an ahistorical and uninformed analysis of the international grain trade. The reporting was superficial and made basic errors about the nature of AWB Limited's role and structure – even politicians at the time seemed to forget that AWB Limited was a private company, slipping into the old terminology and referring to the company as the Australian Wheat Board when that body had ceased to exist nearly a decade before the 2005–06 Cole Inquiry.

Farmers are not necessarily the losers from the low level of public scrutiny of rural policy. In the lead-up to the Commonwealth budget in May 2005, there was public debate over limiting IVF treatments for women aged over forty-two in order to save $14 million per year. Around this time the agriculture minister put out a media release which included the information that the Commonwealth government was spending $4 million *each week* on drought relief. Although not strictly comparable, there was no suggestion that $14 million could be saved in the area of drought relief rather than by restricting IVF services. During the drought at the beginning of this century, a "Farmhand" appeal was set up to raise money for farmers affected by severe drought, even though farmers in these areas were receiving welfare payments on a far more generous basis than other welfare recipients. By May 2005 farmers on drought relief could earn more than twice as much per fortnight as an unemployed person before losing any income support.

The attitude towards the bush could perhaps be summed up as benign indifference. The city pays attention only when issues like the live cattle trade to Indonesia make the headlines or the drought comes to town, as it did in the most recent dry spell. Normally drought happens "out there" and does not manifest itself in the cities except in the form of tight water restrictions. One suspects that the only reason the AWB scandal received such attention was that the media and the Opposition saw an opportunity, not realised of course, to claim a ministerial scalp. AWB Limited's extraordinary delaying tactics, which led to the Inquiry's running for the best part of a year, added to the newsworthiness of the scandal. And it should be remembered that the Inquiry took place in Sydney, so that reporters did not need to get their boots dirty or cope without a decent latte while reporting the story.

There are clearly cultural differences between country and city Australia. Country towns are different from the suburbs. The National Party, One Nation and independents have capitalised on these differences and, although the Nationals have been largely ineffectual in achieving major policy wins for the country in recent Coalition governments, their mere existence appears to provide comfort and earn them support. Apart from the National Party, and more recently the newly influential rural independents, politicians and opinion leaders have not related well to the bush. This is surprising for a multicultural country which has become sensitised to cultural difference based on race and religion, but which seems incapable of showing similar respect for different cultures within Anglo Australia.

I attended three of the ill-fated Murray-Darling Basin Authority (MDBA) meetings in late 2010 and was struck by an apparent lack of respect for rural Australians in general, and for farmers in particular. Doubtless unintentionally, the meetings consisted of suits on stage, talking down to the rural folk. It was death by PowerPoint, with presentations continuing for seventy minutes and no questions being taken until they were done. When questions became challenging, the presenters hid behind the legislation. There seemed to be a lack of sensitivity for the profound impact the plan was likely to have on communities and how it appeared to be a fundamental attack on rural development and a repudiation of previous government support for nation-building irrigation schemes. A key thread running through agrarian ideology is suspicion of the expert and scepticism about the person who works with their head and not their hands. In one meeting we heard a farmer talk about the "university of life" – he clearly regarded his knowledge of his land as equal if not superior to the science being presented by the MDBA. A greater understanding of the culture of rural Australia would have assisted the MDBA in its preparation and possibly resulted in more light and less heat around the draft plan.

The result of the 2010 election drew attention to the needs and demands of rural Australia. Although media commentators in the cities have voiced concern that the influence of the rural independents will result in rent-seeking and sectional subsidies, the public appears to be generally relaxed about the situation. Until the next scandal breaks and TV news and current affairs have some good (or horrifying) footage to run, rural concerns are likely to remain at best second-order issues for the majority of Australians.

Linda Botterill

Tim Mather

In Australia the transformation of city dwellers into tree-changers buying up the fertile country surrounding urban areas has pushed productive farming further into the hinterland. Great swathes of land previously used for horticultural production have been converted into square miles of suburbia, ensuring hot-headed travel for hundreds of thousands of commuters suffering the daily gridlock of crammed motorways.

Imagine the beauty of Europe if Australian city-planning systems had been adopted there. It would be wall-to-wall suburbia, similar to Singapore's waterfront. Instead European planners and politicians astutely realised that the countryside was so important that they would pay farmers to keep fields in agricultural production rather than sell them for urban development.

In biology, different and complex ecosystems develop depending on environmental factors. Thus in high-rainfall, low-lying land, water-tolerant plant systems frequented by water-tolerant fauna develop, with each species working in competition to maintain its niche within the ecosystem.

Australia's political system has developed an agricultural community that has the seeds of its own destruction inbuilt. Species such as sheep, with cloven hooves and dentition that cuts off plants at ground level, have been spread across vast tracts of land which every year is inundated with sudden downpours of rain that destroy soils not being held together by plants. Between the 1850s and 1890s most of the western half of Australia was transformed into desert wasteland because sheep destroyed the delicate balance of species previously present. Many species of plant and animal have disappeared as a result of the introduction of cloven hooves to Australia. Camels and kangaroos (soft-footed both) thrive where cloven hooves destroy.

Beginning with terra nullius, which enabled white Australians to ride roughshod over the incumbents, we now have something similar in the mining industry, where miners fly in from all points of the compass and dig their holes for a week or two before returning to "civilisation" for R&R. Brian Burke's legacy to Australia should extend to his granting fly-in fly-out status to Argyle mining in the Kimberley. Once this was granted, all mining companies requested the same rights. We now have a situation where third-generation Pilbara residents are growing up in communities that lack even regular dental care, let alone physiotherapy or medical services. When Charles Court enabled the development of iron-ore mines in the Pilbara during the 1960s, it was on condition that the miners simultaneously developed town sites. The government, in return, developed other infrastructure, such as schools, hospitals and communications. All those conditions are now gone and remote communities suffer the consequences. Blessed be the name of Brendon Grylls, who in 2008 was elected on the back of his "royalties for the regions" policy.

But back to biology. Australia will always need to feed itself. Logically, it should reserve sufficient productive land and ensure a more reliable rainfall on that land. What brings rain? Trees. In *Collapse*, Jared Diamond argues that destroying trees is the first step toward societal collapse. Australia has destroyed a greater percentage of its forests than any other nation still in existence. The Easter Islanders destroyed all of their trees but didn't live to tell the tale.

Diamond offers Australia as an example of a modern nation likely to collapse because of its agricultural practices. There is little evidence that our modern crop of political or agricultural industry leaders is heeding his warning.

As a veterinarian, I have been fascinated by the recent change in attitude to biological systems in Australia. A previous generation of vets was responsible for the eradication of bovine brucellosis, pleuropneumonia and tuberculosis. This generation has seen the introduction of Newcastle disease, fowl plague and equine influenza, to name but a few. So what has changed? One thing has been the role of the veterinary profession in agricultural communities. Once the Department of Agriculture's vets would regularly visit all the farms in their district and discuss current problems. They would also meet farmers socially in pubs or banks or post offices. As these facilities disappeared, so did the interactions. Not only did the veterinary services disappear, but so too did the agricultural advisers and land agents. As a direct result of the demise of ancillary services to farmers, the incidence of disease and weeds on our lands has increased. Diagnosis of infestations is delayed, and the cost of eradication grows exponentially. An outbreak of ovine brucellosis in Tasmania in the 1970s was fought successfully for less than $10,000. Recently Johne's disease in sheep has spread beyond eradication at an exponentially greater cost. The recent 2007 outbreak of equine influenza cost more than $100 million to eradicate, without counting the cost of community disruption and angst.

Yet the solution to a fair share between country and city is now apparent. First, ensure that each ecosystem is appropriate for its environment. For example, don't grow rice and cotton where there is no water, don't place hoofed animals where there are no plants. Do keep cities on as small a land footprint as possible, so that the energy and resources spent on travel for the majority of commuters are minimised. Do provide services to rural communities, so that centres of population remain smaller but spread apart. Any centres of population should be accommodated on land not useful for food production. Trees should be planted on higher ground and on steep valley edges to control erosion. Tropical and temperate rainforests depleted in previous decades should be replaced by a patchwork, with grazing land in between, so that forestry and grazing can co-exist to the mutual benefit of both.

But if no such changes are made, country folk should not worry too much – they will still be feeding themselves long after the city folk have starved.

Tim Mather

Bernard Salt

Judith Brett has effectively updated one of the most profound cultural stories of the Australian continent and people: the divide – real or imagined – between city and bush. The concept of the "fair share" is presented by Brett as a reimagining of a previous generation's concept of the "fair go." But whatever term is used, the theme is much the same. The tension between city and bush has defined Australia, certainly since the late nineteenth century. By my measure, around half the Australian population was located in the regions at federation; the proportion today is less than 25 per cent. What has emerged, and Brett makes exactly this point, is not just the burgeoning of the capital cities but a new urbanesque life-style on the non-metropolitan coast. It's not that Australians have eschewed the bush; it's just that other, more attractive lifestyles have emerged. As many Australians now live on the coast outside a capital city – in places such as the Gold and Sunshine coasts – as in inland regional cities and towns.

Of course, at federation, when most people lived in regional Australia and Ballarat was the tenth-largest city in the Commonwealth, the bush ruled. At the time Australians very much identified with romantic characters from the bush: the Man from Snowy River and Clancy of the Overflow. Consider some of Banjo Paterson's powerful verse from the 1890s: "And I somehow rather fancy that I'd like to change with Clancy / Like to take a turn at droving where the seasons come and go." This was a city clerk's lament about wanting to live Clancy's life on the Overflow. No city clerk makes such a lament today. If there is daydreaming going on, it might be about going surfing up or down the coast. No one in today's popular culture wants to exchange city for country life. Or at least not for a country life located beyond a two-hour tree-change belt that accommodates city folks' weekenders.

It's hard to find any positive imagery about life in rural Australia in the twenty-first century. The only images of rural life that make the nightly television news tend to revolve around the disasters of bushfire, drought and flood. The popular television series *SeaChange*, which first screened in 1998, had a plot that involved a city escapee (Sigrid Thornton) fleeing not to the flat wheatbelt country but to the pretty coast. Nevertheless, Thornton's love interests were never any of the local yokels – only fellow city escapees. City sophisticates in love in a non-metropolitan setting rate better than do similarly situated locals. Indeed, the locals in this series were variously presented as either simple or naive.

And this is my point about the city's perception of life beyond the big smoke. Even the television news is more often than not presented against a big-city skyline, as if to say that this is the epicentre of a state. Why are there no Clancy-of-the-Overflow pop-culture exemplars in modern Australia? Are there no redeeming lifestyles in any part of the Australian continent beyond the weekender orbit of the capital cities? Why is it not possible to see the lives and lifestyles of attractive, financially successful and – damn it – downright sexy young people not in South Yarra or Double Bay, but in Wagga Wagga, Barcaldine, Clare, Narrogin or Echuca? Is it because twenty-first century Australians believe that anyone with get-up-and-go has got up and gone from rural Australia?

This is not how the British or indeed the Western Europeans see things. In such places there is a social cachet associated with living in the counties that abut London, or in the Loire Valley or Provence. Not in Australia. The settlement of the Australian continent from a series of coastal ports that were culturally and economically connected to the Old Country has proven to be a demographic template difficult for the nation to shake. Perhaps Clancy's era of the late nineteenth and early twentieth centuries was in fact an aberration. Deep down, "colonial" Australians still regard the capital city as being the local outpost of truly metropolitan sophistication. This worldview is reinforced by the increasing connection of capital-city airports to global cities. There is also the decidedly 21st-century lifestyle choice of "fly-in fly-out" workforces. What is fly-in fly-out if not an openly displayed contempt for life in the provinces, let alone the remote regions? Australians would rather fly in fly out ad infinitum than commit to nation-building. The question for the Australian nation and people is this: will future settlement patterns pan out? I suspect that, given the reluctance of the Australian people to invest in permanent settlements in the interior, and the slow and modest population gains being made by regional towns, this issue of the city–bush divide and fair share or fair go – or fair whatever you want to call it – will define the Australian continent and people for decades to come. There will be no resolution of the fair-share debate until there is significant demographic reweighting of the Australian continent in such a way as to diminish the cultural impact of the city.

Bernard Salt

Judith Brett

Country and city are catch-all terms, terms of cultural and geographic location, and of economic and political interest. I used them to structure *Fair Share* because I wanted to write about broad patterns of political argument and broad national policy frameworks. However, it is abundantly clear that in a continent of the size and climate of Australia there are many different countries, many different regions, many different rural areas with their own experiences of the past hundred years or so and their own future potential, or not. Some rural towns and regional areas are thriving and others are just hanging on; but in some cases, as Eric Knight sadly concludes, parts of regional Australia may well be beyond rescue. They are simply too remote. For others, their economic purpose has gone, such as the fettler and drover settlements along the Queensland rail routes which John van Tiggelen describes. European Australia has a short, thin history, with many rural communities lasting scarcely two generations, if that. Yes, parts of rural Australia were always in crisis, as the optimism of the settlers foundered on the realities of soil and climate. This is a part of our history we need to understand; it is a warning against both too much optimism and against the nostalgic belief that we should try to preserve everything. It asks us to disaggregate the catch-all terms of the country or the bush and develop more locally focused policies and understandings.

Jon Altman argues convincingly that indigenous Australians are now at the centre of any contemporary debate about the future of non-metropolitan Australia, with 23 per cent of the continent under some form of indigenous control and much of this in areas of high conservation value where indigenous people are already supplying important environmental services. One could add a cultural dimension to this argument. Aboriginal artists have given settler Australians new ways of understanding the continent, the arid inland in particular, showing beauty and meaning where settlers once saw little of worth.

The Aboriginal-English use of the word "country" is part of this contribution, and it is destabilising the older meanings and associations I was mainly concerned to elaborate. The prime intent of my essay is historical, to set out for contemporary readers what the country once meant for Australians and how this shaped government policy. For most of this history, Aboriginal people were marginal to the debate. It is clear they are no longer so.

Nevertheless, there is still explanatory life in the country–city divide as it has been historically understood, as indicated by comments from both Linda Botterill and Tim Mather on failures of communication with farmers. Botterill observed the suited experts' failure to communicate effectively with the rural folk at the Murray-Darling Basin Authority meetings; and Mather notes the disappearance of Department of Agriculture vets from rural communities, as well as of agricultural advisers and land agents, and the consequent difficulties in communicating quickly with farmers about pests and disease. The lack here is not of information, nor of expert knowledge, but of professionally trained people able to communicate effectively with people in rural communities. This experiential gap in understanding seems greater now than it was fifty years ago.

Bernard Salt goes so far as to claim that it is hard to find any positive imagery of life in rural Australia in 21st-century popular culture. I think this is a little overstretched. True, few contemporary office clerks dream of going droving with Clancy of the Overflow, but then few would have the riding skills; plenty, however, dream of driving round Australia with the camper trailer. And stories about the friendliness and community feeling in rural Australia are regular media fare. The research I reported from Tim Phillips and Philip Smith showed that for many Australians rural life still carried plenty of positive associations. Not every Australian wants to be a metropolitan sophisticate. Salt's comments seem simply to repeat the city's age-old view of the countryside as full of boring, dull parochial people, but this has always in part been in the eye of the beholder.

I have made the decades of the 1980s and 1990s pivotal in the fortunes of the country, giving changes in government policy a key part in this. Governments became more hard-headed about the costs of various forms of support to rural producers and about service delivery, as did various non-government commercial organisations such as banks. And the floating of the dollar and general reduction of tariffs effectively dismantled two of the key ways in which governments had protected rural communities and producers. Just as in the cities, many rural towns lost manufacturing enterprises and jobs in this period. At the time people talked about economic rationalism, by which they broadly meant that economic considerations were put ahead of social benefits. Of course, not all social benefits were discounted, and as Linda Botterill points out, drought relief remained generous, as were some of the adjustment schemes. Australian rural and agricultural policy has always included economic, social and political considerations, though the balance has shifted. During the closer settlement periods political considerations overrode economic arguments; in the 1990s the economists had more purchase. Also important in these last two decades of the twentieth century was increased scepticism about government capacity. The pro-market cause has not just depended on faith in the rationality and capacity of markets but on doubts about the rationality and capacity of governments. Just think Pink Batts.

Eric Knight says that I did not spend enough time on mining. I agree. The focus of the essay was on the interplay between the city and the country, where the country is understood as the settled agricultural areas. In Australia there are clearly other non-metropolitan regions which deserve closer attention, and the causes, nature and impact of the current mining boom would be a good topic for a future *Quarterly Essay*. Knight believes that the modern heart of rural Australia, both economically and socially, is the mining sector. I am not so sure. There is no question of the huge economic benefits of the contemporary mining boom and the prosperity it is generating for people working in the mining regions as well as for other Australians. But because mining relies on a non-renewable resource, it is a particularly unstable basis for long-term settlement. Many of our important inland towns were established as mining towns, but their survival has depended on them accruing other functions. So Broken Hill has become the centre of a thriving art industry, for example. Even in Ballarat and Bendigo the gold lasted only so long, as did their aspirations to be metropolitan cities in their own right, as culturally and economically significant as Melbourne. Given its remoteness from other population centres, and the reliance on a fly-in fly-out workforce, it is fanciful to think that the current mining boom will bequeath a new Bendigo or Ballarat to the Pilbara.

Since *Fair Share* went to press, mining on prime agricultural land has become a matter of public concern. The NSW government has granted exploration leases for coal-seam gas in the Liverpool Plains, alarming farmers and environmental- ists alike. At risk is not just the fertile topsoil, but the underground aquifers. For state governments, mining royalties are one of their few sources of independent income, another of the legacies of federation which continues to shape rural policy. Also at play here is the question of foreign ownership, as the Chinese state-owned mining company Shenhua has been granted an exploration lease.

Knight suggests that foreign ownership is not really a problem, as foreigners have had equity in Australia for over a century. And some politicians have been quick to dismiss public concern as emanating from racism; it would be okay if it were US investment, they say. But this is investment not just by Chinese but by the Chinese state, which is surely a different matter. State-owned Chinese companies, as well as state-backed companies from Gulf states, have also been buying up prime agricultural land and many people are alarmed, arguing that foreign investment in agricultural land, which now includes water rights, needs more regulation. It turns out that the government doesn't even know who owns what out there on the land. The fear is that agricultural companies backed by foreign states will produce the food for export to feed their own nationals. This fear may or may not be well founded, but it shows that land is still basic to people's sense of national sovereignty, and that at base this is about governments protecting the material basis of life. Over the past few centuries, we in the affluent industrialised West have come to take food for granted. City folk may well question agrarianism's faith in the virtue of agricultural life, but they cannot deny its basic premise: that we all need to eat.

Judith Brett

Jon Altman is professor of anthropology in the Research School of Social Sciences at the Australian National University. From 1990 to 2010 he was the foundation director of the Centre for Aboriginal Economic Policy Research, and recently co-edited (with Melinda Hinkson) *Culture Crisis: Anthropology and Politics in Aboriginal Australia*.

Linda Botterill is professor of Australian public policy at the University of Canberra. She has co-edited books on drought policy and the National Party and is writing a book on the life and death of collective wheat marketing in Australia.

Judith Brett is the author of two previous *Quarterly Essays*, *Exit Right* and *Relaxed and Comfortable*. Her books include the award-winning *Robert Menzies' Forgotten People*, *Ordinary People's Politics* (with Anthony Moran) and *Australian Liberals and the Moral Middle Class: From Alfred Deakin to John Howard*. She is professor of politics at La Trobe University.

Eric Knight is a former Rhodes scholar who has worked as an economics consultant to the OECD, the UN Environment Program Finance Initiative and the World Bank. He works for Boston Consulting Group and is a research associate at the ANU Centre for Climate Economics and Policy. His first book will be published in early 2012.

Robert Manne is professor of politics at La Trobe University and a regular writer for the *Monthly*. His recent books include *Making Trouble: Essays Against the New Australian Complacency* and *Goodbye to All That?: On the Failure of Neo-liberalism and the Urgency of Change* (as co-editor).

Tim Mather is a veterinarian with expertise in animal surgery and biosecurity. He has taught at Murdoch University and at the National Institute of Animal Welfare in New Delhi, India, and is currently director of the RSPCA's WA branch and a member of the WA Department of Conservation and Environment's animal ethics committee.

Bernard Salt is a commentator and adviser to corporate Australia on consumer, cultural and demographic trends. He is a partner at KPMG, based in Melbourne. His books include *The Big Shift*, *The Big Picture*, *Man Drought* and, most recently, *The Big Tilt*.

John van Tiggelen was born in Holland, grew up in country Victoria, graduated in science and worked as a tour guide in the Daintree rainforest before turning to journalism. His book *Mango Country: A Journey Beyond the Brochures of Tropical Queensland* was shortlisted for the Colin Roderick Award. He has been writing for the *Age*'s *Good Weekend* since 2004.

SUBSCRIBE to Quarterly Essay & SAVE nearly 40% off the cover price

Subscriptions: Receive a discount and never miss an issue. Mailed direct to your door.

☐ **1 year subscription** (4 issues): $49 a year within Australia incl. GST. Outside Australia $79.
☐ **2 year subscription** (8 issues): $95 a year within Australia incl. GST. Outside Australia $155.
* All prices include postage and handling.

Back Issues: (Prices include postage and handling.)

☐ **QE 1** ($10.95) Robert Manne *In Denial*
☐ **QE 2** ($10.95) John Birmingham *Appeasing Jakarta*
☐ **QE 4** ($10.95) Don Watson *Rabbit Syndrome*
☐ **QE 5** ($12.95) Mungo MacCallum *Girt by Sea*
☐ **QE 6** ($12.95) John Button *Beyond Belief*
☐ **QE 7** ($12.95) John Martinkus *Paradise Betrayed*
☐ **QE 8** ($12.95) Amanda Lohrey *Groundswell*
☐ **QE 10** ($13.95) Gideon Haigh *Bad Company*
☐ **QE 11** ($13.95) Germaine Greer *Whitefella Jump Up*
☐ **QE 12** ($13.95) David Malouf *Made in England*
☐ **QE 13** ($13.95) Robert Manne with David Corlett *Sending Them Home*
☐ **QE 14** ($14.95) Paul McGeough *Mission Impossible*
☐ **QE 15** ($14.95) Margaret Simons *Latham's World*
☐ **QE 16** ($14.95) Raimond Gaita *Breach of Trust*
☐ **QE 17** ($14.95) John Hirst *"Kangaroo Court"*
☐ **QE 18** ($14.95) Gail Bell *The Worried Well*
☐ **QE 19** ($15.95) Judith Brett *Relaxed & Comfortable*
☐ **QE 20** ($15.95) John Birmingham *A Time for War*
☐ **QE 21** ($15.95) Clive Hamilton *What's Left?*
☐ **QE 22** ($15.95) Amanda Lohrey *Voting for Jesus*

☐ **QE 23** ($15.95) Inga Clendinnen *The History Question*
☐ **QE 24** ($15.95) Robyn Davidson *No Fixed Address*
☐ **QE 25** ($15.95) Peter Hartcher *Bipolar Nation*
☐ **QE 26** ($15.95) David Marr *His Master's Voice*
☐ **QE 27** ($15.95) Ian Lowe *Reaction Time*
☐ **QE 28** ($15.95) Judith Brett *Exit Right*
☐ **QE 29** ($16.95) Anne Manne *Love & Money*
☐ **QE 30** ($16.95) Paul Toohey *Last Drinks*
☐ **QE 31** ($16.95) Tim Flannery *Now or Never*
☐ **QE 32** ($16.95) Kate Jennings *American Revolution*
☐ **QE 33** ($17.95) Guy Pearse *Quarry Vision*
☐ **QE 34** ($17.95) Annabel Crabb *Stop at Nothing*
☐ **QE 35** ($17.95) Noel Pearson *Radical Hope*
☐ **QE 36** ($17.95) Mungo MacCallum *Australian Story*
☐ **QE 37** ($20.95) Waleed Aly *What's Right?*
☐ **QE 38** ($20.95) David Marr *Power Trip*
☐ **QE 39** ($20.95) Hugh White *Power Shift*
☐ **QE 40** ($20.95) George Megalogenis *Trivial Pursuit*
☐ **QE 41** ($20.95) David Malouf *The Happy Life*
☐ **QE 42** ($20.95) Judith Brett *Fair Share*

Payment Details: I enclose a cheque/money order made out to Schwartz Media Pty Ltd. Please debit my credit card (Mastercard or Visa accepted).

Card No. ☐☐☐☐ ☐☐☐☐ ☐☐☐☐ ☐☐☐☐

Expiry date /   **Amount $**

Cardholder's name   **Signature**

Name

Address

Email   **Phone**

Post or fax this form to: Quarterly Essay, Reply Paid 79448, Collingwood VIC 3066 / Tel: (03) 9486 0288 / Fax: (03) 9486 0244 / Email: subscribe@blackincbooks.com
Subscribe online at **www.quarterlyessay.com**